6-12

DUE

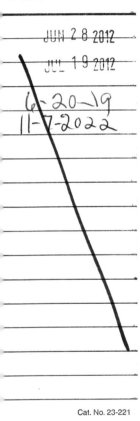

JUN 2 8 2012

JUL 1 9 2012

6-20-19

11-7-2022

Cat. No. 23-221

Mysteries OF THE Mummy Kids

BY Kelly Milner Halls

Darby Creek Publishing

This book is dedicated to Tanya Dean, an editor of extraordinary talents; to my daughters, Kerry and Vanessa, and their cousins Doug, and Jessica, who keep me wonderfully "weird;" to the King Family of Kalamazoo—a minister mom, a radical dad, and two of the cutest girls ever to visit a mummy; and to the unsung heroes of free speech—librarians who battle to keep reading (and writing) a broad-based proposition for ALL Americans. I thank and salute you all.

—KMH

Cataloging-in-Publication

Halls, Kelly Milner, 1957-.
Mysteries of the mummy kids / by Kelly Milner Halls.
    p. ; cm.
ISBN-13: 978-1-58196-059-4
ISBN-10: 1-58196-059-X
Includes bibliographical references (p.) and index.

Learn about child mummies from the Incan and other ancient civilizations around the world, plus a Civil-War-era mummy from the United States.

1. Mummies-Juvenile literature. 2. Human remains (Archaeology)-Juvenile literature. 3. Incas-Antiquities-Juvenile literature. [1. Mummies. 2. Human remains (Archaeology)] 3. Incas-Antiquities.] I. Title.

GN293 .H35 2007
393.3 dc22
OCLC: 70696777

Text copyright © 2007 by Kelly Milner Halls

Cover image © Werner Forman Archive/Greenland National Museum

Published by **Darby Creek Publishing**
7858 Industrial Parkway
Plain City, OH 43064
www.darbycreekpublishing.com

Printed in the United States of America

2 3 4 5 6 7 8 9

Acknowledgements

I would like to acknowledge the invaluable assistance of some of the foremost mummy experts in the world in creating this book and making it as accurate as possible, from a writer's (as opposed to an expert's) point of view. Many thanks for the interviews and e-mails to:

Dr. Johan Reinhard   *Dario Piombino-Mascali*
Dr. Guillermo Cock   *Dr. Elizabeth Wayland Barber*
Julie Scott   *Dr. Victor H. Mair*
Mandy Aftel   *Dr. Niels Lynnerup*
Dr. Johan Binneman   *Clare Milward*
Dr. Peter Pieper   *Dr. Douglas W. Owsley*

Also, thank you to Dr. Zahi Hawass, Heather Pringle, and James Deem for their contributions via their remarkable books, and to dozens of others by way of their professional publications in print and online. Thank you.

-KMH

CONTENTS

MUMMIES AND KIDS

Mummies. I saw my first one almost forty years ago as a kid growing up in Friendswood, Texas. When I was about ten years old, my friend sent me a postcard from Mesa Verde National Park in Colorado. "I saw this real *live* mummy," he had scribbled on the back. But what I saw on the glossy card was undeniably dead.

Looking at that image scared me. It also made me a little sad. But I couldn't take my eyes off it.

Who was this person? I thought. *How did he live? How did he die? And how did he wind up being a mummy?* Those unanswered questions were what had made me feel scared and sad. Somehow it just didn't seem right to put this person's picture on a postcard without telling me something about him. He wasn't some make-believe creature. He had been, after all, a living human being.

Twenty years later, I visited Mesa Verde, a once-vibrant community carved out of the face of a sandstone cliff. Around A.D. 600, the creative and brilliant Anasazi people—who were native to what centuries later became Colorado, New Mexico, and Arizona—created a timeless treasure. Remembering the postcard, I thought, "What's so scary about this?"

I found out that the first mummy at Mesa Verde was discovered in 1889 and that many well-preserved mummies were eventually found. They had been buried in graves that had been carefully closed and sealed. Recently, most of the Mesa Verde mummies were quietly reburied, as is only right. But I never forgot that postcard. And I never stopped wanting to know more about who these mummified people once were.

Mesa Verde gives visitors a look into the lives of the Ancestral Pueblo people, known as the Anasazi, who made it their home for more than seven hundred years, from A.D. 600 to A.D. 1300. The cliff dwellings were deserted suddenly, perhaps because of drought or disease. The mystery of their disappearance may never be solved.

Today the National Park Service protects Mesa Verde's four-thousand-plus known archaeological sites, including six hundred cliff dwellings. These sites are some of the most notable and best preserved in the United States.

Mysteries of the Mummy Kids is my way of finding the answers to all those questions I asked my parents as I looked at that postcard, transfixed. It's my way of reminding myself (and anyone else who reads the book) that mummies are fascinating, but they are not simply empty husks or "scary" objects.

When we gaze at a mummy—whether it's the Yde Girl from Europe or Egypt's boy king, Tutankhamen, who ruled an empire—we are looking at a real person who once lived on Earth. We're studying what's left of that human being. Like all people who walk this Earth, they had dreams and fears, hopes and disappointments. They loved, they hated, they lived— long before they died and were pre- served for future generations to see.

An unidentified man holds a small child mummy found at Mesa Verde by strings tied under its shoulders.

What Is a Mummy?

Before we explore the kid mummy mysteries mapped out in this book, it's important to understand how mummification happens. One biological fact is extremely helpful. About sixty percent of an adult human body is made up of water, and the body of an infant is composed of seventy percent water. Our blood is about eighty-three percent H_2O.

Water is essential to life and to the decaying process—and lack of water contributes to a body's mummification. Most of the time, the water that remains in a lifeless body helps bacteria to grow and thrive long enough to eat, or decompose, the flesh on the bones. It's part of nature's recycling system. But every now and then, the water vanishes so quickly that bacteria can't survive long enough to do their job. In that case, a body may become mummified.

Moisture escapes the body in one way or another—on purpose by being methodically dehydrated or by accident through evaporation.

Natural Mummification

In some cases, mummification is accidental—an unplanned occurrence. For example, if bodies are laid to rest in a frosty cave with arctic winds drawing moisture out of the subzero air, decomposition of a body might not take place. The water might evaporate, leaving a body stiff and leathery but not decayed.

When conditions are hot and dry, the fluids within a body also evaporate quickly, like a loaf of bread left unwrapped on a kitchen counter. Those conditions can cause natural mummification, too.

Mummification by Man

Once people discovered that bodies sometimes become mummified by accident, they sometimes tried to preserve the bodies of their loved ones on purpose. In some cases, as with the mummies of Egypt, people used chem- istry to try to duplicate the natural conditions that mummified bodies. They packed the bodies in salt in order to draw the water out. Then they sealed the dry skin with oily resin to keep bacteria out. In other cases, they tried to copy the dry cave-like conditions that made mummification possible.

Some early people even chose to preserve only the skin and bones of their loved ones and used other natural materials such as grasses and resins to create a replica of the dearly departed.

Cultures that chose to mummify their dead often did so as a tribute to the beloved or important people among them or as a means to provide them with a useful body in their afterlife.

5

South American Mysteries

For decades, anthropologists and archaeologists—scientists who study human life—have been searching the South American landscape for clues to solve all kinds of ancient mysteries. How did the native South Americans live in distant days gone by? And how did they die? By investigating long-buried mummies, artifacts, and other evidence, scientists are able to answer many of these questions. Amazingly, some of the clues were left by mummified children.

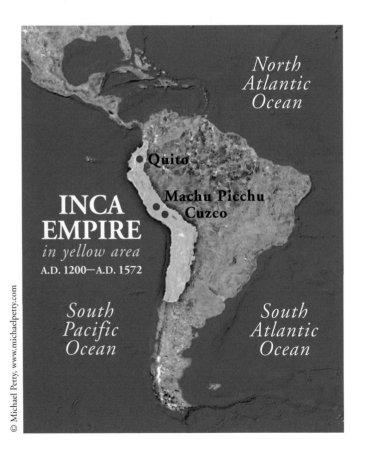

North Atlantic Ocean

Quito

Machu Picchu
Cuzco

INCA EMPIRE
in yellow area
A.D. 1200–A.D. 1572

South Pacific Ocean

South Atlantic Ocean

© Michael Petty, www.michaelpetty.com

Who Were the Incas?

Five hundred years ago, nearly ten million Incan people lived in Tahuantinsuyu, the Land of Four Quarters. Its borders spanned a 2,400-mile region, north to south from the Andes Mountains of Colombia to Chile, and west to east from the Ecuadorian coastal desert to the inner-continental Amazonian rainforest.

The Incas expanded their empire through battles and conquest, but they did not wipe out the villages or the people. Instead, they embraced the conquered people's cultures and incorporated many of their customs and traditions into the Incas' ways.

The Incas did not keep written records, but they did speak a common language, Quechua, which every newly conquered citizen was required to learn. They worshipped various elements of nature, such as the sun and mountains, and offered sacrifices of goods, animals, and humans—including special children—to keep those gods satisfied.

6

Many Incan roads still exist today.

At its most successful point, the Incan Empire was the largest nation in the Southern Hemisphere, with an impressive 14,000-mile network of roads connecting the empire's far-reaching regions. Cuzco was the capital of the empire, and the Emperor and his court spent most of their days in its lavish palaces.

Money was not the currency of the Inca civilization. Incas traded work, not coins, for the things they needed: woven goods, livestock (for wool and meat), vegetables and fruits from the valleys, as well as potatoes and grains from the mountain farms. Gold and silver were highly valued and were molded by artisans into statues large and small for the wealthy and powerful leaders.

The one activity all Incas had in common was weaving. Rich and poor alike wove handspun yarns into fine textiles with patterns that are still duplicated by modern Incan relatives today. Each village had its own pattern that identified its members. That tradition also continues.

The reign of the Incas came to an end in the mid-1500s when the Spaniards—who *did* use gold and silver coins for money—discovered the Inca nation and its rich natural resources. Unlike the Incas, they were set on wiping out Incan traditions as they conquered with force. The Spaniards, called *conquistadors*, tolerated little resistance, destroying as many visible signs of the Incas' religion as they could and often building Catholic churches where Incan temples once stood.

Modern-day Incan descendants weave colorful textiles using the same patterns as their ancestors.

Today the Incas' descendants, as well as historians, anthropologists, and archaeologists, work hard to honor the Incas and to keep their memory alive for generations to come. They carefully issue permits and monitor the explorers who retrieve priceless artifacts. That way the evidence of Incan history isn't available only to private collectors and instead is on display in public museums. Professionals are hired to care for and exhibit the precious items for all the world to see.

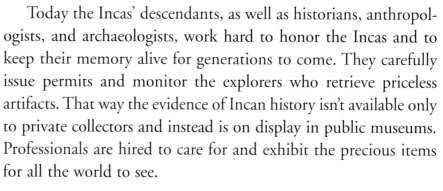

Modern descendants of the Incas in Peru's Chinchero community are proud that the ruins of the last Emperor's country estate are still visible in their village.

7

EL PLOMO BOY OF CHILE

This was the perfect Incan boy, blemish free. Called El Plomo boy (for Cerro El Plomo, the peak on which he was discovered in 1954), the Incan child brought honor to himself and his family by being selected to join the mountain gods.

No one knows for certain, but experts believe this boy and other children of the Incan Empire were sacrificed to ancient gods to ward off bad weather or natural disasters, to improve the health of the Emperor, or to better the Incas' odds in war. The Incas had no written history, but according to Spanish records, called chronicles, the sacrificial cere-

Cerro El Plomo, the mountain peak where El Plomo boy was discovered and for which he was named

mony was known as *capacocha*. In El Plomo boy's case, passing from this life to the next seems to have been relatively painless. Researchers believe that he was given a fermented corn drink called *chicha*, that he fell asleep, and that the frigid cold on the high mountain caused his heart to stop beating.

For five centuries, El Plomo boy's frozen, mummified body waited to be discovered, 5,340 feet up in the Andes Mountains, above Santiago, Chile—17,700 feet above sea level. Wrapped in a colorful, woven blanket, his arms adorned with copper bracelets, his hair neatly braided in more than two hundred rows, the Incan boy was between seven and nine years old when he closed his eyes for the last time.

World-famous mummy-finder, mountain climber, and anthropologist, Dr. Johan Reinhard believes that the below-freezing mountain temperatures preserved the child's lifeless body until some anonymous treasure hunters found it five hundred years later.

Today, forensic anthropologist Dr. Silvia Quevedo Kawasaki is responsible for caring for the mummy at the Museo Nacional de Historia Natural in Chile. According to Dr. Quevedo, El Plomo boy was "exceptional." In NOVA's documentary film, *Frozen in Heaven*, she said, "You can still see it—the energy in him. His face looks very peaceful. He passed from sleep to death without realizing it."

(left) The feathered headdress, black wool threads covering his face, copper bracelet, alpaca-and-vicuna-wool tunic, and embroidered moccasins were part of an ornate costume worn by El Plomo boy at the time of his death.

(below) El Plomo boy now rests in the simplest of his native clothing, appearing as if he is asleep. The rows of nearly 200 braids are still intact.

© Museo Nacional de Historia Natural

Dr. Quevedo explains that El Plomo boy's feet were weathered and callused, indicating a long and difficult journey before he came to eternal rest. This is not surprising, says Dr. Reinhard. The Incan Empire was vast, stretching 2,400 miles from Colombia to Chile. The Emperor would have received the boy, a national hero, in the capital city of Cuzco, and the trek from his home village to the city could have been great. The final stretch from Cuzco to his final resting place took him many miles further. By the time the boy finished the climb up Cerro El Plomo, his fingers would have been blackened by frostbite—an effect of the biting mountain cold. He'd worked hard to complete the journey that would cost him his life but would earn him a promised place with the gods.

www.paredsur.cl

© Museo Nacional de Historia Natural

The rocky tomb of El Plomo Boy atop the mountain

9

Every few years, Dr. Quevedo is responsible for examining El Plomo boy, who is now safely at rest in a protective sub-zero environment. Maintaining such frigid conditions is crucial, because a body can continue to decay at temperatures that are only a few degrees above zero. So the mummy's new home must be kept very cold.

According to Dr. Quevedo, El Plomo boy's smell before and during each examination is her first clue to his condition. "He has a characteristic smell caused by changes in body fat," she told NOVA. "Although it's a strong, penetrating smell, it's a good one. As doctors, we're guided by smells, by touch, by sensitivity. Everything available to us is a valid resource."

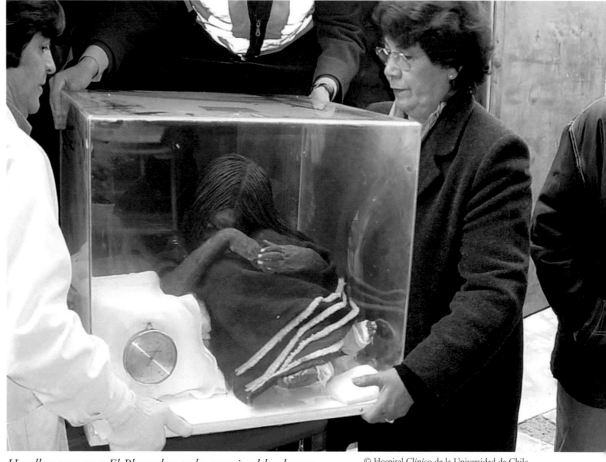

Handlers transport El Plomo boy to be examined by doctors at Hospital Clínico de la Universidad de Chile.

Today, the child wears only the simplest of his native clothing. But more than fifty years ago, Chilean newspaper reports described a boy draped in splendor. Fabric woven from homespun vicuna and alpaca yarn was used to create his black tunic and the gray, blue-green, and red blanket wrapped around his shoulders. Embroidered moccasins made of dark leather covered his callused feet. Black wool threads covered the boy's face, which was painted with vivid red and yellow dyes. An ornate headdress sat on top of his head, and two fabric bags dangled from his neck. Inside one bag were his baby teeth, nail clippings, red wool, and bits of his own hair. Inside the other were coca leaves—a gift for the gods he was to join.

El Plomo Boy's Miniature Companions

Not far from the boy, inside his burial sanctuary, were two figurines of an alpaca and a vicuna, both cousins of the common llama. One was made of gold and the other of silver.

A stunning silver figure of an Incan girl, dressed in fine wools with a headdress of fire-colored feathers, was also found in El Plomo boy's tomb. The figurine was made of several pieces of pre-shaped sheet silver, according to the Metropolitan Museum of Art in New York (where it was on exhibit in the spring of 2006). The pieces were joined together in what may have been a process similar to modern-day soldering—using hot, melted silver as glue.

Fabric was wrapped around the tiny figurine and secured with a miniature sash and tassels at the waist. A mantle, or blanket-like wrap, of woven vicuna wool was draped around her body and held in place with two silver pins unique to Incan women and, therefore, a sign of its gender. A colorful border made the mantle bright and distinctive. An adornment of woven cord with bits of shell tied to each end rested around the figure's neck. A fiery red-orange headdress of tropical bird feathers completed the figure's attire, outfitting her in splendor to accompany the honored boy.

The alpaca was a valuable animal to the Incas, providing food, fuel, and transportation, as well as fine wool that was reserved for royal clothing. A statue of this important animal was found in El Plomo boy's burial sanctuary.

© Museo Nacional de Historia Natural

Just as El Plomo boy had been dressed in splendor for his death, the miniature female statue found with El Plomo boy was also beautifully adorned in preparation for its journey to the gods.

11

WHAT DID INCAN CHILDREN DO?

© Wildland Adventures, Inc.

By comparing the journals of various Spanish explorers, we can piece together what may be accurate accounts of Incan children's lives. However, it's difficult to know if the writings of the Spanish witnesses were fair or accurate, because they didn't always understand the culture they were observing. Even so, based on what was written, some information about the life of a typical Incan child has been generally accepted.

Babies, it was written, were bathed and bundled at birth, but were seldom held until they outgrew their tiny cribs. Once they did, the toddlers were put in pits in the earth, which were used as playpens. There, they could safely learn to walk, work, and play. Older siblings probably helped their parents care for younger sisters and brothers, teaching them to farm, weave, and tend to the family's animals.

Children went to work as young as six or seven years old. Work was an important part of all Incas' lives, but recreational activities, such as playing flute music and simple games, were common, as well.

Some Incan girls were selected early in life to be candidates for special duties, which included *capacocha*, the Incan practice of human sacrifice (usually of "perfect" children), or marriage to important royal family members. The Emperor and other leaders handpicked the *acllakun* ("chosen women") for their beauty and purity. The girls were often from wealthy or important families. They lived a pure lifestyle together in temple-like homes known as *acllawasi* until their sacred duties were decided, usually between the ages of twelve and fourteen.

Most Incan parents believed their daughters would have better, easier lives as acllakun. Those adults who didn't feel the capacocha duties were right for their daughters married them off at an early age, which made the girls ineligible for this higher calling.

Unlike the girls, Incan boys were not selected months, or even years in advance. Instead, they were chosen as the need arose, often from normal Incan households. They were not taken away to live in separate housing. In order to ensure their purity, the boys were hand-picked just before their sacrifice was to be offered, usually before they were ten years old.

Very few Incan children were chosen as sacrifices for their Emperor or country. Most of them lived normal lives, working hard to help their families survive.

(top) Modern-day Peruvian children still resemble their ancestors in their physical features and their daily activities.

Andean flute music was an important part of Incan children's lives.

12

JUANITA: THE ICE MAIDEN OF PERU

For forty years, El Plomo boy was South America's most remarkable Incan mummy. But when Dr. Johan Reinhard scaled the northern face of Mount Ampato in Peru in early September 1995, a new chapter was added to the ever-expanding story—thanks to a mummy known as "Juanita."

For five years, the volcano Nevado Sabancaya had been spitting ash on the surrounding peaks, including Ampato, turning the deep, white, packed snow black in places. The sun baked down on the dark layer of ash, and, because dark colors absorb heat, the snow pack under the dark ash began to melt. When the peak had absorbed enough water, a piece of the mountain broke loose. Buried within that piece was a delicate mummy bundle that Dr. Reinhard would soon discover.

Anthropology and mummies weren't part of Dr. Reinhard's plans for that 1995 mountain trek. He and his climbing partner, Miguel Zarate, were making the dangerous hike for another reason: to photograph Nevado Sabancaya's eruption. They scaled the mountain without any pack burros or excavation tools.

While making their way up the steep face of the peak, winding their way through sharp, towering ice spindles and loose gravel, Reinhard and Zarate spotted a type of grass that did not grow at such heights (20,400 feet above sea level)—a species of grass that had to have been carried in from a much lower altitude. On this summit Reinhard and Zarate discovered the remains of a platform, a place Incan holy men had built to present offerings to the mountain gods. When Reinhard saw just a hint of a bright-red tropical feather and bits of crushed Incan pottery scattered downhill from the summit, he knew the discovery could be much more than just patches of grass.

Almost immediately, the two men unearthed an extremely rare golden female figure on which a miniature feathered headdress sat. Soon they found another female statuette, this one made of silver. They knew that artifacts like these meant this was the resting place of a mummy. But where was it? And how well was it preserved?

Then, they saw what, at first glance, looked like a compacted fabric bundle.

From a distance, Dr. Reinhard and his climbing partner could not identify this bundle, but as they came closer, they saw the face of Juanita, the Ice Maiden.

"Maybe it's a climber's backpack," said Zarate.

"Maybe it's a climber," Dr. Reinhard responded, half-joking because he knew this was a very treacherous climb.

Slowly, carefully, they walked toward the object, all the while collecting scraps of ancient fabric and other artifacts, including two cloth bags filled with maize (corn) and rare shell fragments. Eventually, they were face-to-face with the owner of these treasures: a five-hundred-year-old teenager—Juanita, the Ice Maiden.

Because the cloth that protected her face had been torn away, the Ice Maiden's face had been exposed to the sun and the open air, causing irreparable damage. Dr. Reinhard's heart sank, knowing so much had been lost. But when he tried to lift her, he was encouraged. The mummy weighed about ninety pounds because most of it was still caked with a layer of ice. Her face was damaged, but her still-frozen body might yet be preserved.

The discovery of these rare gold and silver figures was evidence that Dr. Reinhard and his climbing partner were near a mummy's resting place.

Dr. Reinhard discovers Juanita, the Ice Maiden.

Remember, Dr. Reinhard had not climbed Mount Ampato to search for a mummy. He had not requested nor received the special permits required by the government of Peru to rescue ancient treasures. He had not planned on moving such fragile, heavy cargo so far. Dr. Reinhard knew he had to make a decision. If he left the maiden mummy to the face more weeks exposed to the sunlight, her secrets might never be revealed. So he emptied his backpack and tried to wedge her inside.

Once he had the mummy secured in his pack, Dr. Reinhard struggled to his feet and began the wobbly hike back up the mountain, and eventually, back down. With ninety extra pounds strapped to his back, at an altitude where oxygen levels are only half what they are at lower altitudes, hiking wasn't easy. In fact, it was nearly impossible. As daylight escaped them, Reinhard and Zarate had to set Juanita down and hike to camp without her.

Dr. Reinhard barely slept as the night hours ticked by. At dawn, he made his way back—a thirteen-hour hike from base camp—to where he'd left the mummy, while Zarate hiked down the mountain to get a burro. When the two reunited, they and Juanita went back down the mountain, onto a public bus (where they placed their precious cargo in the under-carriage area), and finally to the Catholic University Museum in Arequipa, Peru.

Later, when Dr. Reinhard returned to Mount Ampato with a permit and a fully outfitted team, he found two more children—a younger boy and a younger girl. Both had been damaged by lightning strikes and were found with their afterlife possessions. They may have been companions or servants for the Ice Maiden, Juanita.

15

Who Was Juanita, the Ice Maiden?

Like El Plomo boy, Juanita was one of the chosen—a perfect, pure child selected by officials of the Incan Empire, including the Emperor himself, to live with the gods. But she was about fourteen years old when she made her final journey up Mount Ampato, according to experts at Johns Hopkins University Hospital in Washington, D.C. They carefully performed sophisticated CT-scan procedures (like 3-D X-rays) on May 13, 1996.

Medical experts confirmed she'd lived a healthful life. She had no signs of malnutrition or illness and had good, healthy bone growth. Apart from a skull fracture—the final blow that may have brought a speedy end to her life—she had suffered no previous injuries and had no obvious struggles. She had lived a life of ease, probably as an *aclla* ("chosen woman") in an *acllawasi*, where all these girls lived.

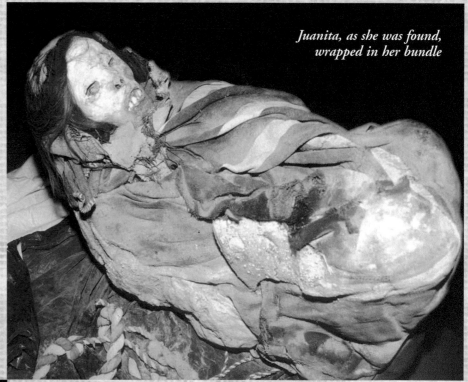

Juanita, as she was found, wrapped in her bundle

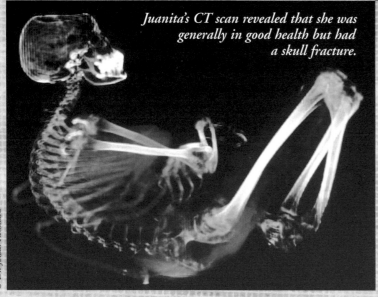

Juanita's CT scan revealed that she was generally in good health but had a skull fracture.

Her station in life was made obvious by the clothing and accessories buried with her. A bundle found in her final resting place was carefully opened and documented by photographs and drawings. Experts, including William Conklin from the Textile Museum in Washington, D.C., were on hand to care for and protect the ancient fabrics. Clinging to the fabric, almost microscopic in size, were pollens from seventeen different plants.

Personal belongings filled the pouch, including what may have been hair from Juanita's first haircut, nail clippings, a piece of carved shell strung on a piece of yarn or cord, a belt, and a cloth bag. A second cloth bag covered with feathers contained coca leaves—just as was found with El Plomo boy—a gift for the gods.

16

© Dr. Johan Reinhard

Juanita's head cloth tore when her bundled body tumbled down the mountain.

This fine red-and-white shawl was found draped over Juanita's shoulders.

© Dr. Johan Reinhard

Slowly and cautiously, the experts worked to peel back Juanita's ceremonial outfit. First, they thawed and removed the woven mantle of gray-and-white-striped alpaca wool. In its folds were more personal belongings, including another bag of coca leaves, balls made of human hair, some string, and a piece of shell. Once the mantle was removed, a fine red-and-white shawl was revealed, woven of alpaca wool and draped over Juanita's shoulders.

Juanita's head cloth had been damaged when she tumbled down the face of Mount Ampato, but it had been elegant. It was dark brown edged by brighter shades of gold, the kind of head cloth worn only by important young women. It was originally held in place over her face by a *tupu*, or metal pin. A second tupu held the mantle closed around her body, and a third fastened the fold of her dress.

Her long ponytail had been tied to her waistband with a single thread, suggesting someone had helped her dress for this final ceremony. More tupus, made of an alloy of gold and silver, were attached to a cord that was woven in a diamond pattern. Tied to each of the pins were miniature animals carved of wood, including what appeared to be a fox or a dog.

The dress, or *acsu*, Juanita wore was wrapped tightly around her body and secured by a corded belt and two more tupus. William Conklin estimated the cloth for the wrap dress to be approximately eight feet long. The dress was brightly banded in stripes of plum, yellow, red, and orange. It was wrapped around and around Juanita's body before it was pinned.

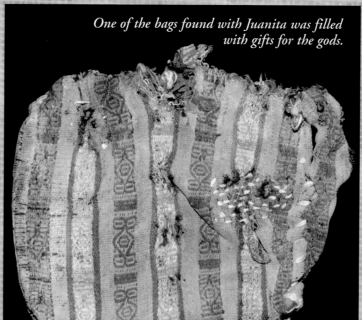

One of the bags found with Juanita was filled with gifts for the gods.

© Dr. Johan Reinhard

Clutching the dress, fingers frozen by mountain temperatures and time, was Juanita's left hand. Inside her stomach was her last supper that had consisted of hearty vegetables. Like El Plomo boy, she also may have drunk chicha before falling asleep. The experts concluded that the meal had been eaten six to eight hours before she drew her last breath.

17

SARITA OF SARA SARA

In September 1996, a year after his discovery of Juanita, Dr. Reinhard returned to Peru fully prepared to repeat the success on Mount Ampato, this time on the Andean peak of Sara Sara, which was known as a *huaca*, or sacred place. Eleven burros carried food, supplies, equipment, and personal items. A team of archaeological experts climbed with him, eager to search for and find more Incan mummies.

Two days' climbing landed the team 15,000 feet above sea level at the base camp where the tents and equipment would rest. But they had to climb higher. A smaller camp was established at 18,000 feet—near where Dr. Reinhard had found a tupu way back in 1981.

With great reverence and respect, the international team made a burnt offering of coca leaves to the mountain gods, an appeal for success. After struggling with the symptoms of *hypoxia*, or lack of oxygen, which included headache, sick stomach, light-headedness, difficulty breathing, and lack of sleep, the climbers switched to their more scientific efforts.

On the first day of the search, Dr. Reinhard's co-director, José Antonio Chávez, found four tupus—three in perfect condition and one damaged by the elements. It was a good sign and a good way to decide where to start digging. *Scrape, scrape, scrape.* The sound of shovels and pick axes removing ice and gravel replaced the peaceful howl of the mountain winds. The search was taking place in several different, but nearby, places.

18

The dig team works atop the Andean peak of Sara Sara.

The team excavates the Sara Sara mummy.

"Diablos!" Dr. Reinhard said. Translation: "Devils!" According to NOVA, he said this each time he encountered an especially stubborn stretch of frozen mountain.

"Diablos!" his associates and students echoed, teasing their leader.

At last, in the distance, there was an excited cry for "Johan." An artifact had been found—then two, then five, and then seven. The bundles looked modest at first glance, like mud-soaked laundry. But inside were pure silver and gold—literally. José Antonio cared for the rare artifacts, guarding them in secrecy until he could deliver them to the Catholic University in Arequipa, Peru (where Juanita is on display).

A dig member holds one of the female statues found with Sarita that indicated the mummy was female.

© Dr. Johan Reinhard

José Luis, a member of the dig team, made the next discovery. The face of a six- or seven-year-old Incan child slowly emerged from the earth. She was found with three female statues, proof that she was also female. Her knees were pulled up to her chest, and she was wrapped in a stunning black-and-white wool shawl. But because she was buried too close to the surface of the sun-baked eastern face of the mountain, decay had set in. She was not well preserved. The team continued to free her and the artifacts buried with her, but they hoped another mummy would also be found.

Unfortunately, their efforts to discover more surprises were fruitless. One mummy would have to do.

The team members made their way down the mountain with a tiny body frozen in so much soil and ice that it weighed one hundred and twenty pounds. Along the way, joyful villagers from Quilcata, Peru, met them. Everyone agreed to name her Sarita, "little Sara," after the Andean summit on which she was found.

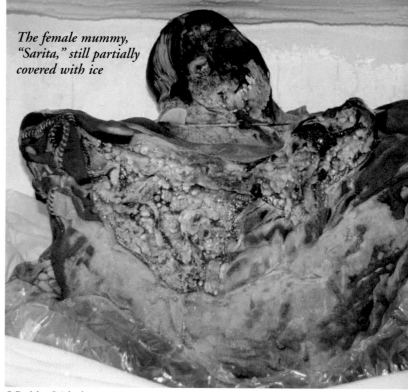

The female mummy, "Sarita," still partially covered with ice

© Dr. Johan Reinhard

19

CHILDREN OF LLULLAILLACO

For five hundred years, the bodies of three sacrificed children remained frozen in silence, undetected. A six-year-old girl, a seven-year-old boy, and a fourteen-year-old maiden lay buried just beneath the surface of the highest Incan site ever found so far. They were discovered by Dr. Reinhard and his team of American, Argentine, and Peruvian experts in March 1999 on the 22,000-foot peak of Argentina's Mount Llullaillaco. After three days of braving seventy-mile-per-hour winds and stinging cold, dozens of priceless artifacts were discovered.

Based on her fine clothing and the items discovered with her, experts believe that The Maiden was an aclla, or "chosen woman."

Honored as heroes and future gods before they made their final climbs, these children ate the finest foods, wore the finest textiles, and may have even met the Incan Emperor himself. Their parents probably loved them and grieved their loss, but also felt proud of their young ones. According to their beliefs, these children would be sacrificed to help protect the Incan people and to keep the empire safe. In return, the chosen children would live out eternity in the company of heavenly beings.

THE MAIDEN

Because she was older than the other two mummies—approximately fourteen—this one was called "The Maiden" by Dr. Reinhard and the Museo de Arqueología de Alta Montaña (MAAM) in Salta, Argentina. Unlike a younger female mummy who was facing west, The Maiden was facing east, leaning back, her legs crossed, her arms resting on her stomach, as if she were sleeping.

Her light-brown acsu was tied at the waist with a bright-colored woven belt. A gray-and-red mantle was wrapped around her shoulders and was held in place by a silver tupu. Her dress was further adorned by a dangling set of ornaments. The Maiden's dark, long hair was woven into dozens and dozens of small braids. In fact, according to Dr. Reinhard, the braids were pressed into her frozen skin and left her face marked by the patterns.

"Probably," says the MAAM exhibit text, "this young woman was an *aclla*, or 'virgin of the sun,' and lived in the *aclla huasi*—'House of the Chosen Women'—as did Juanita, perhaps."

Placed in her tomb were wooden spoons, cups made of wood, a comb, ceramic pottery, textiles, six bags containing food and coca leaves, and the largest figurine of them all: a miniature female cast in silver with a fine headdress of white feathers.

20

THE GIRL STRUCK BY LIGHTNING

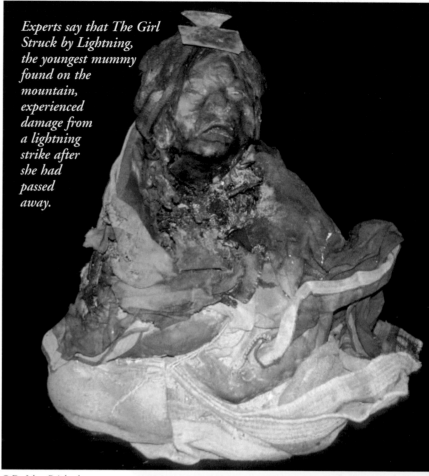

Experts say that The Girl Struck by Lightning, the youngest mummy found on the mountain, experienced damage from a lightning strike after she had passed away.

© Dr. Johan Reinhard

The youngest of the three mummies now rests at the MAAM, too. Known as "The Girl Struck by Lightning," she took her last breath long before her tiny body was marred by nature. But even the power of lightning couldn't erase her story.

Like most young Incan mummies, this six-year-old girl probably was given chicha to drink before she was lowered, possibly deeply asleep, into her burial tomb. In a little more than two hours, her small body was frozen solid, according to Dr. Reinhard.

When she was found, the girl still looked as if she were sleeping. She wore a pale-brown dress with a colorful woven belt and a brown mantle that was pinned with a silver tupu at the chest under her chin. Her head was once covered with a smaller, dark, wool blanket. A light-brown blanket embroidered at the edges with bright colors was wrapped around her whole body.

Two braids of straight, black hair were pulled back from her face. Above them, she had worn a headband adorned with gleaming silver. (It was later removed when she was prepared for preservation.) Evidence showed that her skull had been bound when she was an infant, reshaped to seem more pointed, as was the practice of her people.

Carefully placed in her burial tomb were carved wooden cups called *keros* for drinking, wool bags called *chuspas* full of food and coca leaves, an animal skin bag that may have contained her own hair clippings, a comb made of thorns, pottery, sandals called *ushutas*, moccasins, and miniature figures meant to represent people and animals that would be important for the young girl's eternal journey.

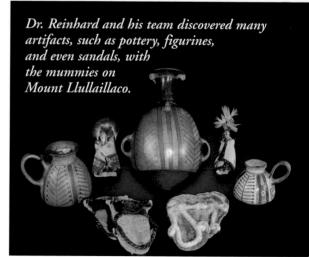

Dr. Reinhard and his team discovered many artifacts, such as pottery, figurines, and even sandals, with the mummies on Mount Llullaillaco.

© Dr. Johan Reinhard

21

THE BOY

The only boy in this trio was probably about seven years old. He looked very small, sitting with his legs pulled up against his chest, his face snuggled against his knees as if he was taking a nap. He was dressed in a red tunic and wrapped in a brown-and-red mantle. Unlike the girls, his hair was cut short, as was customary with prominent Incan males, and his head was adorned with a white feather on a wool headband.

Decorated leather moccasins covered his feet. A white, animal-hair anklet was tied in place above each foot. And his tiny hands were frozen in fists.

Near the boy's body were miniature human and animal figures made of silver, gold, and shells. They were miniatures of a wealthy Incan man, leading the finest alpaca herds, protected by a fine necklace of shells placed in a semi-circle around the objects. Two pairs of sandals were also near the boy.

© Dr. Johan Reinhard

The Boy of Llullaillaco, whose dress reflects prominence, lays almost as if asleep against his knees.

© Dr. Johan Reinhard

Dr. Reinhard found tiny figurines depicting a wealthy Incan man and his herd of alpaca near the boy mummy.

22

An Interview with
Dr. Johan Reinhard, Mummy-Finder

Dr. Johan Reinhard kneels next to Juanita, the Ice Maiden.

© Dr. Johan Reinhard

Dr. Johan Reinhard is a high-energy explorer and an expert at anthropology, mountain climbing, foreign languages, and photography. And he's made some of the world's most remarkable mummy discoveries. For more than twenty years, he's studied Incan dig sites in search of archaeological information. I asked him some questions about the Incan mummies.

Halls: Can you tell us how the Incas selected which children were to be sacrificed?

Dr. Reinhard: We can't be completely sure, because the Incas didn't keep written records, so you have to compare eyewitness accounts with the facts you find on the ground. The Spanish chronicles offer eyewitness sources, but they have been criticized for being hard on the non-Christian Incas. They've even been accused of stealing information from other chroniclers, which was done all the time five hundred years ago. Plus, none of the Spaniards actually observed the ritual. No Spaniard ever *saw* it. So you look for consistencies in more reliable reports, and you compare those with details you find on the ground. Forensics tops historical data every time. That said, the children were selected for their physical perfection and their purity.

Halls: Why would parents allow this to happen to their children?

Dr. Reinhard: It's important to understand that the Incan parents thought they were sending their children on to much better, easier lives than the lives they'd been living. They were going to live with the gods. And there is evidence their children's lives did greatly improve after they were chosen. There was a change in their diets, for example— much better food. If the parents did not want their children to be selected, they simply married them off at an early age.

Halls: How long did it take for the kids to go from their homes to their ultimate destinies on the mountainsides?

Dr. Reinhard: They walked great distances. Even from their villages to Cuzco, where the Emperor lived, must have required many days, if not weeks. Then they went from Cuzco to the mountain summit, making offerings at all the sacred places along the way. It could have been a pilgrimage of several months to a year.

Halls: What was the most remarkable moment for you?

Dr. Reinhard: That would be the moment I saw the face of the Llullaillaco Maiden. She was so amazingly well preserved, for an instant I thought she was alive. I felt a flash, like an electric current run through my entire body. I had always wanted to look into the face of an Inca, though I knew it was impossible. And yet, there she was. The culmination of twenty years of hard work lined up in the perfect moment. It was as if my wish had been fulfilled.

The Mummy Bundles of Tupac Amaru

South American archaeologist Guillermo Cock first went to Tupac Amaru, a sun-baked shantytown named after the last great Incan leader, six miles east of Peru's capital of Lima, in 1999. There, he found more than 1,200 families who had been driven from their mountain homes by decades of civil war and drug-related power struggles between guerrilla armies and government-sanctioned troops.

There wasn't much to see—no running water, no bathroom facilities, no electricity. But beneath the makeshift houses, beneath the humble elementary-school playground, lay thousands of the region's mummified Incan ancestors, five hundred years dead.

The mummy bundles were Tupac Amaru's secret buried treasures, hidden in the second-largest Incan cemetery in Peru (now known as Puruchuco). The villagers were not happy to see the excavation team come and disturb their fragile community. They feared being moved out by the government and expected the dig team to loot the graves and run off with any treasures. Guillermo eventually earned their trust by hiring some of the local people to join the dig and become part of the excitement.

The two-year dig began on the dry, warm playground, as kids with soccer balls and jump ropes looked on. Guillermo's quest was to set the bound mummies free, including hundreds of mummified kids.

According to Guillermo, making mummy bundles was the Incas' special way of preparing the dead for their journeys into

24

(top) Workers excavate the remains of mummy bundles near Puruchuco, the second-largest Incan cemetery in Peru.

(bottom) Wrapped within the large mummy bundles were the mummy and items that he or she might need in the afterlife.

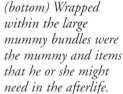

the afterlife. The Incas believed souls could communicate with the living from the next world. So they placed special, cherished items between layer after layer of ancient woven textiles, as they wrapped the bodies of their departed loved ones for burial.

Each bundle was five or six feet long. Some weighed as much as five hundred pounds. Some mummies were buried alone, but others were wrapped as groups. Those group bundles were called *falsas cabezas*, or "false-heads," because each one had a false head attached to make it seem a little more human in shape. Some of the artificial heads were adorned with wigs, headdresses, or masks, but none had faces. As many as seven bodies were hidden inside a bundle, and each person had trinkets of his or her own.

From 1999 to 2001, more than 1,200 mummy bundles (also called funerary bundles) containing nearly 2,400 mummies and 50,000 artifacts were carefully removed from the dry ground of Tupac Amaru. Each body had been buried during the same seventy-five-year time period about five hundred years ago. Almost half of those mummies had been children under the age of twelve.

So, Who Was Tupac Amaru?

The town of Tupac Amaru was named for the last Inca, or holy leader, of the Incan civilization, who was murdered by Spanish soldiers in 1572. Many leaders before him had fought or negotiated with the Spanish warriors occupying their country to save their people. But promises made by the invaders were often empty.

By the time he became the Incas' holy leader, Tupac Amaru had seen many crimes against his people. The Pope, whom the Spanish considered their holy leader, had ordered the Incas to convert to Christianity. Those who resisted did not survive. Angered by the cruelty, Tupac Amaru ordered Christian landmarks destroyed and tried to remind his brothers of their own spiritual roots.

The Spanish captured Tupac Amaru, put him in prison, and ordered him to convert. But even as they were teaching him the rules of baptism, they were planning his death. They accused him of a murder he did not commit and convicted him without a trial.

In Cuzco, a crowd of his followers surrounded the platform built for Tupac Amaru's beheading in the heart of the city. One witness said their impassioned cries "deafened the skies." But Tupac Amaru remained brave and

proud. He calmly raised his hands to silence the grieving people and asked to say good-bye to his children. With dignity, the children climbed the platform to give their father one last hug.

In his last statement, Tupac Amaru said, "Mother Earth, witness how my enemies shed my blood." Then, with one swift stroke, the Spanish executioner cut off his head and held it up for the horrified crowd to see. Tupac Amaru was buried in a Christian church's graveyard—built on the Incan monument to the sun that once housed the mummies of his ancestors.

A painting depicting Tupac Amaru

25

THE KID AND THE COTTON KING

One man inside a very heavy falsa cabeza bundle at Tupac Amaru was nicknamed "The Cotton King," because he was padded with nearly three hundred pounds of raw cotton. (In the days of the Incas, cotton was brown and sandy in color.) Special trinkets, such as rare Spondylus shells, as well as weapons and sandals worn only by the very rich, were wrapped with the Cotton King within the seven layers. But tucked into the fifth layer was what may have been the Cotton King's saddest legacy: the mummified body of a child.

Here is a look, layer by layer from the outermost to the innermost, at what was found with the Cotton King.

LAYER ONE

Spondylus shells–These were quite rare, because they came from the faraway coast. Only important people had them tucked in their funerary bundles.

Guinea pigs–We see them as fun, furry pets. The Incas saw them as fun, furry menu items. They were probably placed in the layers to be sure the loved one would have something to eat.

LAYER TWO

Bird feathers–Colorful feathers from a macaw were tied together at the stem and placed here.

LAYER THREE

Sandals–Footwear was unusual in Incan culture. Only high-ranking members of the ancient society were allowed to wear them.

Huaracas–If you've ever had a sling shot, you know the best use for *huaracas*—firing off projectiles, such as stones or hardened seeds. Made of wool and leather, Incan people also wore them as headdresses, wrapped four times around their heads.

©Rick Spears

LAYER FOUR

Unidentified feathers–These feathers were so rare, even modern archaeologists don't quite know what they are.

Mace–This star-shaped weapon placed in the fourth layer of the mummy bundle suggests the Cotton King was also a warrior. The sharp, pointed head was made of a copper alloy. The handle was made of a black hardwood called *chonta*.

LAYER FIVE

Child mummy–DNA testing has yet to confirm whether or not this child was the son or daughter of the Cotton King, but some people believe it must have been a child of great importance to the man. No one knows for sure who died first: the Cotton King or the child.

Cactus spine comb–This instrument was wound together with its wooden handle using string. It may have been used to help make fabrics.

LAYER SIX

Cotton padding–Three hundred brown-and-tan-colored pounds of it

LAYER SEVEN

Corn–Buried with the Cotton King was a generous supply of corn, or maize. Corn was part of the Inca death ritual.

Feathered headdress–Only important people in Incan society were allowed to wear feathered headdresses. One more clue that the Cotton King may have been an important tribal leader.

© Pilar Olivares/Reuters/Landov

Dr. Guillermo Cock describes the remains of an excavated mummy bundle.

A South American Mummy Curse?

Whether mummy excavations take place in Egypt, China, or Peru, one thing is almost certain. If a tomb or burial ground is opened, someone will probably say, "Beware of the mummy curse." Dr. Guillermo (Willy) Cock's excavation at Tupac Amaru was no exception.

Villagers of Tupac Amaru blamed the scientists for some bad luck that happened soon after they started digging up the mummy sites. When Dr. Cock and other members of his team developed a mysterious and very persistent cough, Peruvian villagers cried, "Curse!" They feared the spirits were angry because of the disruption. But when a young boy in their village died, they were convinced. (According to Dr. Cock, the child very likely died of natural causes, probably tuberculosis.)

A simple analysis revealed that the true cause of the "mummy cough" was raw human sewage that seeped through the ground from the villages. Because there was no modern plumbing, the sewage from the village was endangering the mummies in the first place. The moisture was destroying what years of burial in the dry, Peruvian soil had preserved. And it was the same sewage that caused the cough.

CIVILIZATION'S OLDEST MUMMIES
(AND THEY AREN'T IN EGYPT)

The Incas' Andean mummies were "accidentally" preserved by nature, but some of their ancestors—the Chinchorros, a primitive tribe of fishers—were mummifying their dead on purpose. Thousands of years before the Incas came to power—and long before the ancient Egyptians began the practice of mummification—some natives of Chile used mummification, mostly likely to ease their sorrow. Mummies of rich and poor, old and young, all were a part of this ancient burial ritual.

The oldest mummy that has ever been discovered was near Chile's Camarones Valley and was mummified around 5050 B.C. Like many of the Chinchorros mummies, this one was a child.

Life on Chile's northern desert coast wasn't easy 7,000 years ago. The Chinchorros struggled to survive in the rugged ancient world. As the adults worked hard to survive, the community's infant mortality rate began to skyrocket. One of every four babies did not survive. So, the heartbroken families started mummifying their children, infants, and fetuses.

Why were many of these mummies so young? What caused these tragic deaths? According to archaeologist Bernardo Arriaza of the University of Tarapaca, the answer may be simple—poison. Even today, high levels of arsenic are common in the waters of the region. Arsenic and lead poisoning can be fatal to babies, even before they are born.

Mummified Chinchorro children now rest at Azapa's San Miguel Museum in Chile. Some are so small and fragile that they are placed in special boxes to protect them.

28

© Phillipe Pailly/Eurelios

© Ivan Alvarado/Reuters/Landov

"We've always known that the Camarone (the region where the mummies were unearthed) had a lot of arsenic," Arriaza said in a Reuter's news report on November 27, 2005, "and the first mummies were children."

The process used by the Chinchorros to mummify their dead was unlike any other culture's. First, they carefully peeled the skin from the person's body and set it carefully aside. Then they removed all of the flesh (soft tissue, including muscles) and internal organs. Once the bones were clean, the skeletons were reconstructed, often reinforced with small sticks to make them stronger.

Once the skeletons were complete, the internal organs were replaced with clay duplications. Next, the muscles were replaced with replicas made of plants and sea grasses. Once those changes had been completed, the deceased's human skin was sewn back in place. If any piece had been damaged, sea lion skin was used in its place.

Finally, the modified bodies were covered with a coat of prehistoric paste and then a layer of black manganese (a metallic mineral). These are called the Chinchorros' "black mummies." Later, when manganese was harder to find, "red mummies" were made using red ochre instead of manganese. Next a clay mask meant to resemble the lost loved one was often placed over the mummy's face. Wigs of human hair and clay hats or helmets were also added in many cases.

Almost three hundred Chinchorro mummies have been found. About half of them were mummified on purpose. The other half were preserved by nature, not man, in the dry Atacama Desert.

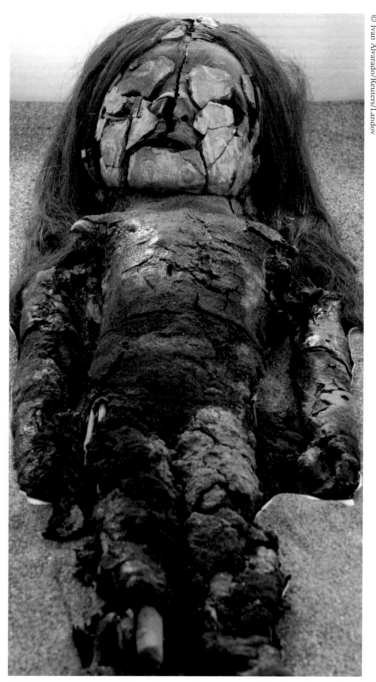

Black manganese is still visible on this mummified Chinchorro baby.

29

MEXICO'S ACCIDENTAL MUMMIES

Before 1958, the living citizens of Guanajuato, Mexico, had to pay a tax on their deceased: one hundred and twenty pesos up front if the person was wealthy, and twenty pesos per year if he or she was not. It was a law, not a request. Skip the payment, and your loved one would be evicted from his or her grave.

But something strange happened when the tax collectors made good on their threat for the first time on June 19, 1865. According to Guanajuato's Web site, the body had mummified naturally in the dry, environment. That presented a problem. What do you do with a "homeless" mummified body?

Answer: You create a museum to house the grave-less bodies—*Museo de las Momias* (Museum of the Mummies). For a very long time, the people of Mexico have honored the deceased and their belief in an afterlife with traditions like *Día de los Muertos*, or Day of the Dead. So setting up the museum was a natural solution.

Between 1870 and 1907, eighty-six more bodies filled its shelves and niches. Today the count is one hundred and eleven and rising, including nineteen children. Girls were mummified holding dolls, mummified infants are held by their mummified mothers, and even premature babies, including the so-called "World's Smallest Mummy," are on display at the Museo de las Momias.

Every year about 800,000 visitors pay to tour the museum, giving the city of Guanajuato a steady source of income. According to museum director Felipe Macias, "The dead of Guanajuato are giving something back to their city."

Mummified children line the walls of the Museo de las Momias in Guanajuato, Mexico.

© Three Lions/Getty Images

30

Mysterious Mummies of Egypt

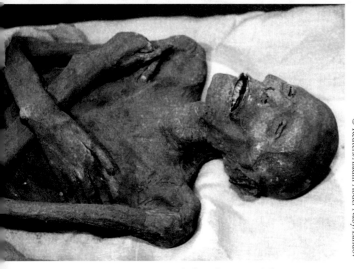

DNA testing proved the identity of this mummy as the Egyptian pharaoh Ramesses I.

© Reuters/Aladin Abdel Naby/Landov

Although the mummies of Egypt are not as ancient as some of the mummies in South America, some are far more famous. When word of the golden riches found buried with Egyptian mummies hit nineteenth-century newspapers, their popularity soared around the globe.

The same factor made the boy king, Tutankhamun, the most famous of Egyptian mummies. More artifacts made of gold and other materials were found entombed with Tut than with any other mummy. But he wasn't the only mummy kid in Egypt.

For centuries, hundreds of mummies of all ages filled dozens of tombs in Egypt, especially in the Valley of the Kings. Their bodies—mummified by priests in preparation for the afterlife—were discovered by explorers and thieves many generations after they had been laid to rest.

In recent decades, many of the mummies have been preserved and protected in their homeland, studied and cared for by experts, including famed Egyptologist and Secretary General of the Supreme Council of Antiquities, Zahi Hawass. Dr. Hawass helps bring royal mummies home to the Egyptian Museum in Cairo whenever he can. Some mummies have been scattered far and wide, excavated by foreign scientists and historians to be put on display in museums around the world. Sadly, others have been stolen by tomb raiders and sold, along with their artifacts, to the highest bidder. These mummies have been lost, perhaps forever.

But sometimes the news is good. For example, in 2003, after DNA testing proved a mummy in Atlanta's Michael C. Carlos Museum was the lost pharaoh Ramesses I (who reigned from 1293-1291 B.C.), the museum's curator, Dr. Peter Lacovara, sent him home to Egypt. Dr. Hawass was thrilled. "We are very happy it will be returned to Egypt where the rest of the royal mummies are," he told *National Geographic News*.

No matter where they rest, these mummies, including Tutankhamun, have a glorious history in common. They were the children of the powerful Egyptian Empire—one of the most notable civilizations in human history. And because of the mummies' careful preservation, their lives will never be forgotten.

KING TUT'S TOMB

If not for the legendary British archaeologist Howard Carter (born May 9, 1874, in London, England), King Tutankhamun and his queen might have remained mysteries forever. If not for the riches of Tutankhamun, Dr. Carter might never have been so famous. Their destinies connected on a November morning in 1922.

Carter had seen evidence of a tomb for Tutankhamun. Another expert, Edward Ayrton, had discovered a burial cup inscribed with Tut's name in 1906. Also found were scraps of gold foil and broken pottery, perhaps spoils of a robbery that had been stashed until the thieves had more time to go back for the rest of the treasure. These clues convinced Carter's wealthy English sponsor, Lord Carnarvon (also known as George Edward Stanhope Molyneux Herbert), to pay for the search.

Authorities granted Carter permission to excavate one remote site in Egypt in 1914, but the onset of World War I delayed his quest. Even after he renewed his search in 1917, Carter's expertise and Lord Carnarvon's money yielded many artifacts—but nothing of Tutankhamun's. With hope and financial support running low, Carter asked for one more chance at a new location in the Valley of the Kings in November 1921, promising to refund the expense himself if he failed.

The experienced archaeologist had been successful in making important discoveries not connected to Tutankhamun. He was well educated and respected professionally by Egyptians and Englishmen alike. Lord Carnarvon agreed to fund one more excavation, and a year later, his faith and investments paid off.

Tutankhamun's tomb lies in the Valley of the Kings among many other tombs of ancient Egyptian royalty.

Archaeologist Howard Carter (left) stands with his financial sponsor, Lord Carnarvon (right).

Hidden amid the rubble of the tomb of another pharaoh, only six feet beyond an abandoned tomb worker's room, Carter found a hidden staircase. After removing centuries of debris, he went down the stairs and into the adjacent hallway. With the light of a mere flickering candle, he saw it—a plastered door marked with what he thought was a royal seal.

Carter sent for Lord Carnarvon and his daughter, Lady Evelyn Herbert. Once they arrived, Carter began to open the massive door. At first, he had only a small peephole chiseled away, barely big enough for a thread of candlelight to sneak through. But even with so small a window, Carter peeked inside to see. "Everywhere, the glint of gold," he wrote in his official papers. By day's end, a wider entrance confirmed the treasure.

Although thieves had looted the antechamber at least twice before Carter made his discovery, hundreds of remarkable artifacts still lined the first room of Tutankhamun's tomb. Three other rooms—a burial chamber, a treasury, and an annex—were also discovered.

A cosmetic jar made of calcite, ivory, and gold with a lion upon its lid was one of more than five thousand artifacts discovered in Tut's tomb.

Once all four rooms had been opened and catalogued, the inventory count rose to more than 5,000 precious artifacts.

According to Zahi Hawass, even with some of the era's best Egyptologists lending their expertise and both hands, it took ten years to fully clear and catalogue the tomb's contents. Keeping such careful records was unusual in the early twentieth century. Hawass says most teams would have rushed in and cleared the space in two to three months. It took nearly three months for Carter to move from the antechamber to the second room, Tutankhamun's burial chamber. He finally opened the pharaoh's tomb on February 17, 1923.

Among the many treasures revealed in Tut's tomb was a small, gold replica of a sarcophagus.

33

THE MUMMY OF TUTANKHAMUN

Some call him the golden king because of the vast stores of treasure found with his mummy. Some call him the boy king because he took his place on the Egyptian throne when he was only eight years old. And some call him the world's most famous pharaoh because his riches have dazzled people worldwide. But the truth is, King Tutankhamun was very nearly forgotten.

The golden death mask of Tutankhamun

Pharaohs who took power after the young king died tried to remove all references to Tutankhamun, his wife, and his father, Akhenaten, from historical records. The teenage king might have remained forgotten if British archaeologist Howard Carter hadn't found him—in another man's tomb. After the discovery of the tomb, Tutankhamun's mummified body remained locked in its royal *sarcophagus*, an ancient decorated coffin, for another three years.

Why the delay? In 1922, Carter had offended Egyptian officials by allowing the tomb to be visited by English onlookers, including dig members' wives. The crowd and noise made the event seem like a circus, rather than the somber viewing of a young, deceased king. Disgusted by the lack of respect, Egyptian officials banished the British team from the tomb. After three years of diplomatic efforts, Carter was finally allowed to examine the mummy itself.

Tutankhamun was laid to rest inside a nest of three beautifully decorated wooden coffins—a box inside a box inside a box. According to Carter's own diaries, the archaeologist finally broke the seal of the third and final lid on October 28, 1925.

Beneath the lid, Carter found what he called a "bespangled" but neatly wrapped mummy "with [a] golden mask of sad but tranquil expression." (The mask was secured to Tut's face with burial resin.) Carter acknowledged the power of silence. "[It] made us realize the past," he said.

Carter surmised that Tutankhamun must have been a tall youth, about six feet from the top of his mask to the bottom of his feet. Three heavy, golden necklaces adorned his throat. And the mummy held a heart-scarab pendant in his hands, his arms crossed on top of his jewelry-covered chest.

Today, we handle mummies and their artifacts with meticulous care, respect, and dignity. Carter's team was not so cautious. Although they understood how rare the materials were, they seem to have been caught up in the rush to bank the valuable treasures. They often forgot to treat the mummy of Tutankhamun with the protection and reverence it deserved.

Howard Carter views the innermost coffin of Tutankhamun's sarcophagus.

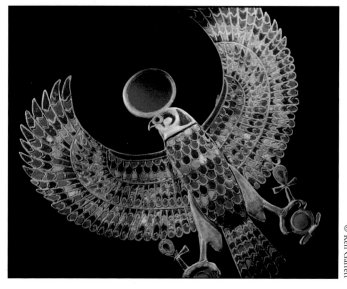

This large gold-and-jeweled necklace was among the many pieces of jewelry found in Tut's tomb.

Linen coverings and outer bandages were wrapped around the body, but the bandages were cut away and destroyed. Resin that was meant to seal the coffins and preserve the boy king had darkened the fabric and made the printed hieroglyphs difficult to read. Carter feared the oily humidity from the same hardened liquid resin might also have damaged the mummy. Considering the damage allegedly done by Carter's team later, that concern seems ironic.

Carter's team found more necklaces, amulets, bracelets, and rings beneath the coated bandages, many of which were also stuck to Tutankhamun's mummy with resin. Others were packed under his body, behind his knees, and beside his hands. A small, flattened circle of gold covered his belly button. Hundreds of priceless items filled the young pharaoh's coffin.

Ten men carried the open sarcophagus out of the tomb. They hoped the scorching Egyptian sun would melt the sticky resin so the jewels could be removed. The team became frustrated when this didn't happen, so they allegedly cut the pharaoh's body into pieces to make gathering the riches easier—but not before the chest cavity was crushed when they tried to pry the gold and gemstones from his mummified skin. They used a hammer and chisel to try to free Tut's death mask, but when that didn't work, the men used red-hot knives to cut through the resin, lift the mask, and reveal what was left of his face.

As a result, it was difficult to determine King Tut's cause of death seventy-five years later when experts carefully examined the body. Dr. Zahi Hawass now guards Tutankhamun's mummy and tomb like a devoted watchdog. He is determined to keep the boy king safe from further harm for generations to come.

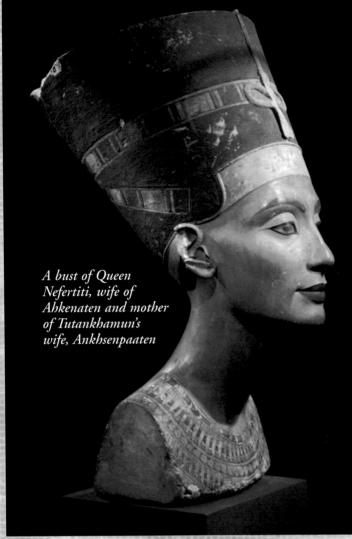

A bust of Queen Nefertiti, wife of Ahkenaten and mother of Tutankhamun's wife, Ankhsenpaaten

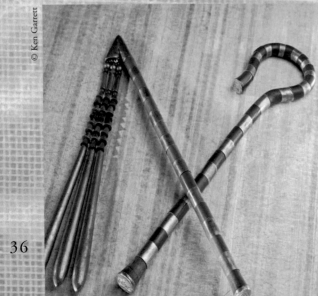

An Eight-Year-Old King?

How can we be sure Tut took the throne at such a young age? Evidence found in his tomb made it clear. Miniature versions of adult pharaoh necessities, such as crooks and flails; bows, arrows, and quivers; beds, desks, and chairs—everything a young pharaoh would need was included. Tutankhamun truly was the Boy King.

Tut's father was disliked because he wanted all of his people to worship Aten, a god that was unpopular with most Egyptians. In fact, Tut's original name was Tutankhaten. He was given that name in honor of the god Aten, as was his half-sister and preselected wife, Princess Ankhsenpaaten. She was the daughter of Tut's father and Queen Nefertiti. Tut's own mother was probably Kiya, a secondary wife of his father. It may seem strange to marry such a close relative, but it was common in ancient Egypt, especially among the royal family.

"Tutankhaten and Ankhsenpaaten would probably have been married to one another at a very young age," says Dr. Zahi Hawass in his book *The Golden King: The World of Tutankhamun*, "for reasons of state [political reasons]. But perhaps they also loved one another."

When the young rulers were crowned, they restored the religion that had come before their father—and took new names to proclaim it. Egypt's eight-year-old king became Tutankhamun, and his young queen became Ankhsenpamun, in honor of the more popular god Amun. With that religion restored, the Egyptian people loved Tutankhamun.

When he died so young and suddenly, probably at age seventeen (in about 1323 B.C. according to the Chicago Field Museum, where some of King Tut's artifacts were on exhibit in 2006), no tomb had been prepared for his body. So his advisor, Ay, gave up his own tomb in the Valley of the Kings to enshrine the young pharoah. King Tut's devoted subjects filled the small crypt with riches beyond compare.

A statue of Ahkenaten, Tutankhamun's father, at the Luxor Museum

Miniature versions of a pharaoh's crook and flail found in his tomb identified Tutankhamun as a boy king.

36

HOW DID TUTANKHAMUN DIE?

For decades, Egyptologists and other historians wondered if the young king died suddenly due to foul play. X-rays taken in 1968 and 1978 revealed two bone chips at the base of Tutankhamun's mummified skull that could have come from a violent blow to the head.

Murder would explain why Tutankhamun's royal tomb wasn't ready for its master. And killing the young pharaoh would certainly make his advisor's (Ay) ascent to the throne much easier. But a sophisticated CT scan in August 2005 that produced 1,700 detailed images put the head wound theory to rest.

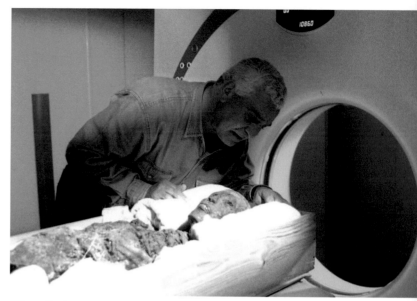

© Reuters/Landov

Dr. Zahi Hawass oversees the CT scan of Tutankhamun's mummy.

The injury was much more visible in the new CT scan, but the images showed no sign of embalming fluid penetrating or leaking through the wound. With that evidence in mind, experts from Egypt, Italy, and Switzerland agreed that the chips happened *after* the young king's death and mummification, probably during Howard Carter's excavation. That doesn't rule out murder by another means—poison, for example. It simply solves the mystery of the fractured skull.

The new images revealed more information about the young king. He was in good general health, judging from the sound growth and strength of his bones and teeth. But Tutankhamun may have had a serious wound on his left thighbone, a break that might also have included an open wound. If infection had set in, it could have killed Tutankhamun quickly and unexpectedly. Experts agree that embalming fluid *did* settle into the broken thighbone, suggesting the break may have caused an open wound. But it is also possible that the embalming fluid fell into a break in the fragile bone and flesh carelessly made by Carter three thousand years after Tutankhamun had been mummified.

How the boy king died may remain a mystery forever, but clues to how he lived are preserved in the more than five thousand artifacts that were discovered. Many of the spectacular pieces are part of the "Tutankhamun and the Golden Age of the Pharaohs" exhibit that has been and will be shown in several major cities around the world, including Chicago, Philadelphia, and London.

GETTING INSIDE A MUMMY

In July 2004, digital imaging experts from California used their advances to reveal the secrets of the mummy of Nesperennub, an ancient Egyptian priest at London's British Museum. Nesperennub's sarcophagus had not been opened since ancient embalmers sealed it 2,800 years earlier. And experts at the British Museum weren't about to change that.

"We don't want to unwrap mummies," said expert John Taylor, who works at the museum's Department of Ancient Egypt and Sudan. "It's very destructive." Using laser scans and special software, 3-D images show the inside of the mummy, layer by layer. This visual experience was viewed by the public on a twelve-foot-tall by forty-two-foot-wide screen.

Thanks to 3-D-stereo glasses, thousands of visitors could look inside the body of the ancient holy man without damaging a scrap of his afterlife linen. In the twenty-two-minute interactive film, they saw his decorative jewelry, his abscessed tooth, his arthritic joints, and even the clay bowl that had been accidentally glued to his head with embalming resin.

Image of Nesperennub produced by SGI. Permission to reproduce granted by SGI/British Museum 2006

High-tech CT imagery allowed the public to see the mummy of Nesperennub without opening his sarcophagus.

What Is a CT Scan?

CT scan is short for computer tomography scan. The word "tomography" is derived from two Greek words: *tomos* meaning "slice" and *graphia* meaning "description." A CT scan is set of computer-generated, 3-D images taken in tiny slices or layers, guaranteeing incredible detail and precision.

The person (or mummy) to be examined lies on a metal surface that moves slowly inside a large cylinder-shaped chamber. The process can take between thirty minutes and two hours, depending on how many images (of how many body parts) experts want to capture.

A CT scan can be used to study many parts of your body, such as the brain, chest, abdomen, arm, or leg. It also can take pictures of body organs and structures, such as the liver, pancreas, intestines, kidneys, lungs, heart, blood vessels, bones, and the spinal cord. Doctors compare "normal" images with a patient's scans to look for problems.

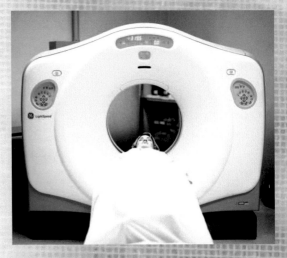

As a person (or mummy) moves through the CT scan chamber, the machine captures many layered images that provide detailed views of different parts of the body.

EGYPT'S "LITTLE ONE"

Some of the California experts who had been involved in the digital imaging of Nesperennub saw an article in the local newspaper about the Rosicrucian Egyptian Museum in San José. They called museum director Julie Scott to ask if she had any mummies she'd like to have digitally scanned. Without hesitation, Scott replied, "Yes!"

The museum had a number of mummies worthy of attention, but the director's thoughts turned almost immediately to the smallest mummy in the collection—a two-thousand-year-old Egyptian child who had never been identified or unwrapped. Affectionately known as Sherit, which in ancient Egyptian meant "little one," this mummy was the obvious choice for a long overdue personal introduction.

SHERIT REDISCOVERED

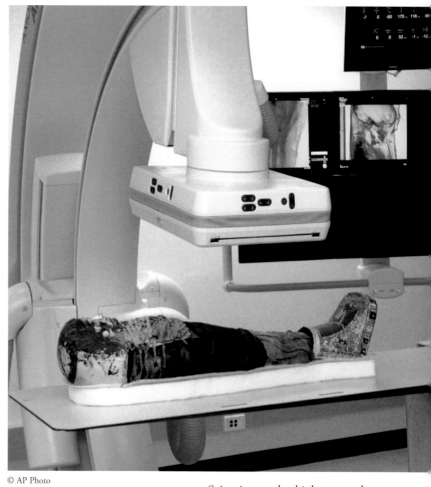

© AP Photo

Scientists used a high-powered CT scanner to help identify "Sherit," the little mummy from the Rosicrucian Egyptian Museum in San José, California.

Using one of the world's highest-powered CT scanners, experts took more than 60,000 images, visual "slices," of the little mummy. (Only 1,700 slices had been captured to better understand King Tut.)

Layer by layer, some of the little mummy's mysteries were revealed. Beneath the mummy's *cartonnage* (hard protective covering of linen or papyrus and plaster) were the traditional linen bandages, or wrappings. Delicately printed on the linen over her chest was the faintest indication of traditional hieroglyphs that should eventually reveal the mummy's real name.

"We know they're there," Scott said. "We can see the patterns on her chest where we would expect her name to be. As we peel back the layers, visually, with careful study, someday we'll be able to read it. It's only a matter of time."

It's a Girl!

Beneath the bandages was a head of curly, resin-coated hair—proof Sherit was a little girl. "Boys," according to Scott, "would have had their heads shaved. All boys' heads were shaved while they were living." The team also found four tiny *canopic* packages (covered clay jars) containing her internal organs, which had been removed and mummified separately.

When the CT scan showed Sherit's skeletal structure, her bones, the mummy's age was scientifically revealed. Doctors and dentists who studied the formation of cartilage and the growth of her baby and adult teeth agreed she died and was mummified at about age five. Her feet, which appeared misshapen at first, were, in fact, normal little feet that had been forced into an odd position during the mummification process.

© Paul Sakuma/AP

A CT scan revealed information about the physical structure of Sherit, which was the basis for this reconstruction of her head.

Most Egyptian mummies' heads are tilted back, their bodies kept horizontal. But Sherit's chin was pressed firmly against her chest, indicating she had been laid to rest in a coffin that was too small. Some theorize that Sherit's family was so grief-stricken by the loss of their daughter that they kept her sarcophagus in the house with them, standing rather than lying down, just to have her memory near.

There are no signs of physical trauma or of poor nutrition. She was in excellent health almost immediately prior to her death. But the mortality rate among weaned Egyptian children was greater than fifty percent. When they had to drink water or other liquids instead of mother's milk, the risk of intestinal illnesses, such as dysentery, could prove deadly. Experts believe this was probably Sherit's cause of death.

In addition to examining the visual images, plastic surgeon Stephen Schendel and some forensic sculptors from Medical Modeling in Golden, Colorado, used exact measurements of the mummy's skull to create a fleshed out bust of what Sherit might have looked like.

"Suddenly this little girl just came to life for us," said Julie Scott. "She was even more real than she had always been."

40

Sight and Scent:
Making Sherit "Come to Life"

The perfect mix of science and technology made Sherit big news. But it took chemist Mandy Aftel to help make her human—and undeniably real. Adding to the sense of sight and touch, Aftel recreated the sweet scent that had been used to anoint little Sherit's burial mask.

Aftel uses natural materials, not synthetics, to create her popular fragrances. She is one of the best in her field, so when the idea to recreate the fragrance popped up, her name popped up, too. Aftel was chosen to reproduce the scent used to anoint Sherit, the five-year-old Egyptian mummy.

Aftel explains, "I did a lot of independent research myself on Egyptian embalming. But the experts had also done a scientific test on samples taken from the mummy to isolate what ingredients were actually used." The test revealed frankincense (also known as olibanum oil), myrrh, and oil of Ben (also known as behen oil, common in the ancient and modern Middle East).

"Based on my research," Aftel says, "I thought there might have been more ingredients. But I wound up making an extremely simple perfume of elements already familiar to me. It was a soft, pretty odor—and an important part of the burial ritual that honored the little girl. I feel confident that I accurately reproduced the original.

"Scent is such a powerful, human experience," she says. "It added another dimension to the whole experience. The rest of what was revealed on the screen was mostly science. This—the scent—was more in line with the arts. It was emotional. And it was real."

What was the perfume called? "Sherit," Aftel says with a smile.

She created a one-of-a-kind fragrance for this one-of-a-kind mummy. No other name would possibly do.

© Mandy Aftel

Chemist Mandy Aftel created a fragrance based on Sherit's anointed burial mask.

*"Sherit,"
the fragrance*

© Mandy Aftel

41

KID MUMMIES OF EUROPE AND ASIA

Many places have their mummies—natural or manmade. Europe and Asia are no exception. But, like the other kid mummy mysteries we've examined from South America and Egypt, they are, in their own ways, unique.

Some, such as northwestern Europe's bog people, were crime victims or criminals. We can't be sure how many people were buried in the bogs, but some experts say they number in the thousands. From infants to the aged, human beings were tossed into the murky swamps, where their bodies became mummified, preserved in amazing detail because of the chemical makeup of the gooey slosh that engulfed them. This is a very different kind of mummy from the ones preserved by the dry heat or cold of their environments.

Others in Eurasia were more like the mummies we have already described. For example, China's red-haired Taklamakan mummies became mummified after they had died of natural causes—preserved by the dry, desert sands. But who they were is a mystery. Where did these tall, European-looking mummies come from? They don't resemble people who are native to China. And why was a mummy baby, found in a grave nearby, not laid to rest in the tomb with his mom and dad?

We'll explore these and other mummies that have been found in Europe and Asia. And we'll examine some of the mysteries of their lives, revealed by mummified postmortem clues.

A rare oasis sits among the vast desert sands in China.

Northwestern Europe's Bog People

After the last Ice Age ended about 12,000 years ago, peat (also known as *sphagnum*) moss bogs began to form in northwestern Europe. Deep pockets of oxygen-starved rainwater rested between mounds of surface soil. The bogs were dark and mysterious places. Ancient people, called Celts, lived nearby, and they built wooden roads across the bogs. The bogs may have been considered holy places.

Eventually people started dropping things into the bogs. Like ancient wishing wells, the bogs were places where people left gifts, hopefully pleasing the gods and bringing themselves good fortune.

Trinkets were not the only items placed in the bogs. Human beings ended up in the murky marshes, as well. We may never know if they were left as sacrifices, punished for crimes, or just buried, as is the standard custom in many cultures. Forensic evidence shows that many had died violent deaths, long before recorded human history. Because of the bogs' composition, these human bodies became mummified—naturally preserved in a soup of chemicals.

To date, more than two hundred bog bodies have been recovered across northern Europe.

A mound of peat moss is set aside to dry.

Sphagnum Science

Sphagnum moss has three qualities that make mummification possible. First, it can hold rainwater in its cells, so it doesn't depend on streams of water to survive, just some occasional rain. Second, sphagnum moss removes much of the oxygen from the water. The less oxygen, the less decaying of a body. Third, when the sphagnum dies, it releases something called *sphagnan,* which slowly turns to humic acid, according to mummy expert Heather Pringle. In her book, *The Mummy Congress,* Pringle says humic acid, along with nitrogen, softens and sometimes slows the bacterial growth that causes decay and decomposition.

"That tends to preserve the soft tissue as well as the hard tissue," she explains. "The skin is dried a little bit, but all the features are preserved." In other words: mummified.

With its many pockets of water and abundant plant life, a bog can hide many secrets, including mummified bodies.

YDE GIRL

With a rope wrapped tightly around her neck, the Yde Girl probably experienced a violent death.

© Gene J. Puskar/AP

She wasn't like the other teens in her village. This sixteen-year-old girl walked with a limp. Her right foot was twisted slightly inward, and her right big toe was swollen from the stress of carrying most of her weight on one side. Her right second toe was callused and hard. One shoulder most likely was a little higher than the other—one hip and one side of her rib cage, too. Her misshapen frame made it impossible for her not to limp. All of these symptoms probably occurred because the girl's spine was curved.

Today, we call this spinal condition *scoliosis*, and medical treatments are available to help ease the symptoms. But in the year 170 B.C., long before modern medicine could explain or help the condition, the ancient people may have considered it a curse—proof that this girl wasn't favored by the gods. Archaeologists call this four-foot, seven-inch-tall person the Yde (pronounced *ee-dah*) Girl.

About two thousand years ago, she was placed in a dank grave—in the bogs near today's province of Drenthe, Holland. No one knows why. Perhaps the village's crops weren't growing. Perhaps the rain hadn't come—or had come with too much force. Maybe a sickness had swept through her area, and the elders felt a sacrifice would restore health.

In contrast to the Incas of South America, Celtic tribal leaders may have sometimes sacrificed the people whom they judged as *less* important to their villages—criminals, the physically disabled, and even people they just didn't like.

We may never know why, but one thing is clear: The Yde Girl met a violent end. A seven-foot-long cord was wrapped three times round her tiny throat and pulled tight with an ordinary slipknot. Half of her head had been shaved of its beautiful, shoulder-length red (or blond) hair. The other half still was still intact when peat farmers accidentally dug her up near the village of Yde in 1857.

For one hundred years, the Yde Girl was kept in a small local museum. Eventually, she was taken to the Drents Museum of the Netherlands, where today she is respectfully cared for by bog body experts.

A sign marks the bog where peat farmers found the Yde Girl.

44

Yde Girl's Face Restored

When the peat farmers found the Yde Girl, they were terrified. They didn't know what to think of this body, and they weren't even sure what to do with it. So they left her there. But before they returned to salvage her body, all but one of her teeth had been stolen, and what was left of her long hair had been pulled from her scalp.

When modern experts took over, all that changed. Ever since she's been under the care of the Drents Museum, the Yde Girl has been valued and protected. She's had the chance to tell her story.

Giving the Yde Girl a human face was one way to give her a voice. So, in 1992, when British facial reconstruction expert Richard Neave was asked to recreate the Yde Girl's face, he accepted the challenge.

When a mummy's skull is well preserved, special artists can make exact copies and sculpt a life-like face using clay or wax. In the case of the Yde Girl, more than one hundred years had caused the mummy to become dry and fragile. So a CT scan was performed to help Neave get the skull replica he needed to produce an accurate look.

Neave's first attempt seemed wrong to him, too small, even for the tiny girl. Experts agreed that her skull might have shrunk in the bog. So Neave made the reproduction fifteen percent larger—and her features came into focus.

"The face that emerged," Neave says, "was a rather unusual one, with small features, wide-set eyes, and a very high, straight forehead."

Neave replaced the red hair with a blond wig, believing the bog had changed Yde Girl's original hair color. And he's not sure her nose is correct. "As with many ancient skulls, the nasal bone was lost," he says. "So the final result shows a nose that is consistent with the other features of the face, but not necessarily accurate."

Dr. Wijnand van der Sanden, former curator of archaeology at the Drents Museum, examines the facial reconstruction of the Yde Girl.

© Drents Museum

45

From his remains, doctors could tell that the Kayhausen Boy had a deformity in his hip, which may have been a reason he was killed.

KAYHAUSEN BOY

Like the Yde Girl, the seven-year-old Kayhausen Boy may have been singled out by leaders in his community because of his physical disability. But because so little is known about this child—no written records were kept or preserved—we can't be sure. We can only guess, based on what little physical evidence we have.

In 1922, farmers in a peat field in Lower Saxony, Germany, found his battered body. The joint where his femur (thighbone) met his hip socket was fused, or stuck together, causing it to be stiff or even locked in place. As a result, he probably walked with an obvious limp and may have even needed a cane. In 100 B.C., this may have made him seem vulnerable and imperfect—each reason enough to make him the choice as a sacrifice back then.

Kayhausen Boy had a cord wrapped around his neck, too, like Yde Girl had. But his killers were even more violent. The poor boy had been stabbed in the neck and in the arm, possibly as he was trying to block the attack on his throat. Before his lifeless body was put into the bog, his arms were tied behind his back, and his feet were tied together with a cape.

For two thousand years, his mummy lay in the bog. After some doctors took possession of the Kayhausen Boy soon after his discovery, they preserved his body in a liquid mixture of alcohol and formalin. The mummy wasn't examined again until 1952, when a new generation of doctors removed his internal organs and intestines and placed them in jars of a similar preservative.

Studies of the sediments in the jar that housed the boy's intestines showed that his last meal had included cereal, fresh fruit, and a kind of wild grass common to his home village at the time.

It's hard to say which set of facts is more painful to consider: what we *do* know about this sad little boy, or what we *don't*. We know he was mistreated and brutally killed. But what we don't know is even more confusing. Why was such a little boy treated so badly? Where was his family? Did anyone even try to save his life? Even if we knew the answers to those questions, we might never understand what he went through and why.

The answers are lost forever in the ancient silence of the bogs. Respectfully cared for at the Landesmuseum für Natur und Mensch in Oldenburg, Germany, the Kayhausen Boy may finally be at peace.

WINDEBY GIRL

Two lives were ended two thousand years ago at a bog near Schleswig Holstein, Germany. In 1952 two bog mummies were discovered: one an adult male and the other a female teenager. The teen mummy came to be known as the Windeby Girl. She took her last breath when she was about fourteen years old.

We'll never know what drove her village, today known as Windeby, to drown the girl in twenty inches of bog water. But their anger was obvious by what she endured during her last day. Windeby Girl was unclothed, fitted with a leather collar, and blindfolded. Her fine blond hair was shaved to the scalp on the left side and was clipped to only one-inch-long on the right.

Some reports say one of her legs was broken before she died. Others say it was injured when peat farmers accidentally dug her up. But there is no doubt about how she passed away. She was purposely drowned in the shallow waters of the mysterious bogs for reasons we may never understand.

In the book, *The Bog People*, author P. V. Glob describes Windeby Girl: "She lay on her back, her head twisted to one side, her left arm outstretched. The right arm was bent in against the chest, as if defensively, while the legs were lightly drawn up, the left over the right. The head, with its delicate face, and the hands were preserved best."

© Horst Pfeiffer/dpa/Landov

Today, she rests on display in a climate-controlled case, along with four other bog bodies in the Landesmuseum near Schleswig, Germany.

The Windeby Girl remains in the same position as when she died in the bog almost two thousand years ago.

Sicily's Dressed-Up Mummies

In the late 1500s on Italy's island of Sicily, the Capuchin Order of Franciscan Monks in the capital city of Palermo made a startling discovery. Not all of the bodies that had been buried in their earthly cemeteries were decomposing. Some were being mummified by nature.

When one the monk's most revered brethren, Brother Silvestro, passed away in 1599, they decided to mummify him on purpose so they could pray to him long after he had moved on to his heavenly reward. The process they used on Brother Silvestro was continued for several decades after his preservation. To be mummified, the body was carefully laid on a bed of loosely woven wire, allowing bodily fluids to escape as the warm, dry winds blew over the remaining bones and soft tissue.

The Capuchin Catacombs are the final resting place for many members of the religious community, including this mummified high-ranking church official.

Once the dehydration process was complete, the mummies were dressed and put on display. Some had even asked ahead of time, sometimes as their dying wish, that their clothes be changed from time to time.

Word of the mummification success traveled quickly, and wealthy citizens all over the island of Sicily wanted to make sure their bodies would be mummified and dressed in fine outfits, too. The Capuchin monks and other burial officials often delivered what the wealthy dearly departed requested, for themselves and for their beloved family members.

The Capuchin Catacombs contain a room dedicated to the mummies of children.

The hallways of the Capuchin Catacombs contain not only mummies but also many skeletal remains.

"Mummification was not always achieved [by that process]," says Italian paleopathologist, Dario Piombino-Mascali, who has spent many years studying the mummies of Sicily. "When it wasn't successful, the skeleton was covered in a layer of straw, and then dressed. In the majority of cases, the head and hands were the only parts exposed."

In time, thousands of lifeless mummies were hung from hooks on walls across the island. Others were on view in open boxes and wall-mounted shelves. Still others sat in chairs or open alcoves. Some reports suggest eight thousand mummies are preserved at the Capuchin Catacombs alone. Among the immortalized are rows and rows of children.

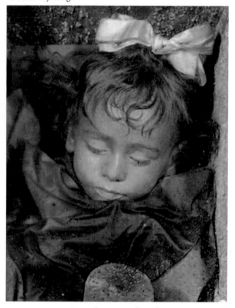

Rosalia Lombardo was so well preserved in about 1920 that she has not changed much at all.

"There is a section dedicated to the children whose bodies are suspended in wall niches," says Piombino-Mascali. Like the adults, some of the children are actual mummies; others are skeletal remains dressed in their best outfits.

Perhaps the most disturbing is the haunting-alive-looking mummy of the young Rosalia Lombardo, who rests in St. Rosalia's Chapel. Almost perfectly preserved through a mysterious process created by Dr. Alfredo Salafia in about 1920, she was only two or three years old when she died. Although the secrets to Dr. Salafia's method died with him, Piombino-Mascali suspected that Rosalia was "intra-arterially injected." In other words, embalming fluids may have been injected into her veins, turning her into a doll-like mummy, rather than a dry, withered mummy like those on display nearby.

Two kid mummies are posed in a rocking chair atop a ledge.

AN INTERVIEW WITH PALEOPATHOLOGIST DARIO PIOMBINO-MASCALI

Paleopathology is the study of ancient diseases. Experts in this field can tell whether or not an ancient person was healthy or sick before he or she passed away. They investigate clues about how ancient people lived, what diseases affected them, and how they died. Dario Piombino-Mascali has studied for years in order to prepare for a career in this field. He is currently a student at the University of Pisa in Italy.

He has made it his life's work to study and document the Capuchin and other mummies on the island of Sicily. I asked him a few questions about his work and the mummies he grew up with.

(top left) Paleopathologist Dario Piombino-Mascali stands next to some of the remains at the Capuchin Catacombs.

(top right) Mummies hang on a wall dedicated to priests.

(middle right) The skeletal remains of a mother and her daughter stand together, still dressed in clothing from the time in which they lived.

(bottom) This hallway of the catacombs is dedicated to male mummies only.

Halls: How many of the bodies in the Capuchin Catacombs are actually mummified and how many are skeletal at this point?

Piombino-Mascali: I haven't counted all the bodies at Palermo yet, but there are thousands. Many of them have undergone only partial mummification, but many others are beautifully preserved. A reasonably high number of people are skeletonized, but I believe this happened (in many cases) as far back as when the bodies were placed in the "special rooms" in order to allow the escape of bodily fluids. Mummification was not always achieved [by that process]. When it wasn't, the skeleton was covered in a layer of straw and then dressed. In the majority of cases, the head and hands were the only parts exposed. Bare skulls are rather common, too.

Halls: How many children were laid to rest in the catacombs?

Piombino-Mascali: There are a good number of children, although very few compared to the number of adults. There is a section dedicated to the children whose bodies are suspended in wall niches.

Halls: Did any of the mummies move you more than others? If so, why?

Piombino-Mascali: The children's room is definitely the most moving section. These quiet children seem to be in the wrong place. Have you seen the pictures of such section? Rosalia Lombardo, the best-preserved

mummy at Palermo, is not in that section, but rests in the St. Rosalia Chapel.

Halls: As a student of archaeology and pathology, which facts surprised you, if any?

Piombino-Mascali: It is stunning to see how some mummies are still so well preserved after so much time. I am surprised how the Capuchins could reach such a result with a rudimental, yet efficient, method of drainage.

Halls: Why did you decide to study these individuals?

Piombino-Mascali: I decided to study the Sicily mummies (not only Palermo, but also the other collections scattered around the island, as well) when I finished my degree in biological anthropology and archaeology at Pisa. But I have known about these collections since I was little, as my family originates from Sicily. I was inspired to pursue the study by my tutor, Professor Gino Fornaciari, who is a pioneer in mummy studies.

Halls: What do you plan to study next?

Piombino-Mascali: I am cataloguing the subjects (the mummies) and describing pathologies visible on very detailed inspections. I am trying to establish whether each individual was mummified naturally or artificially. I am planning to continue my historical, medical, and anthropological research.

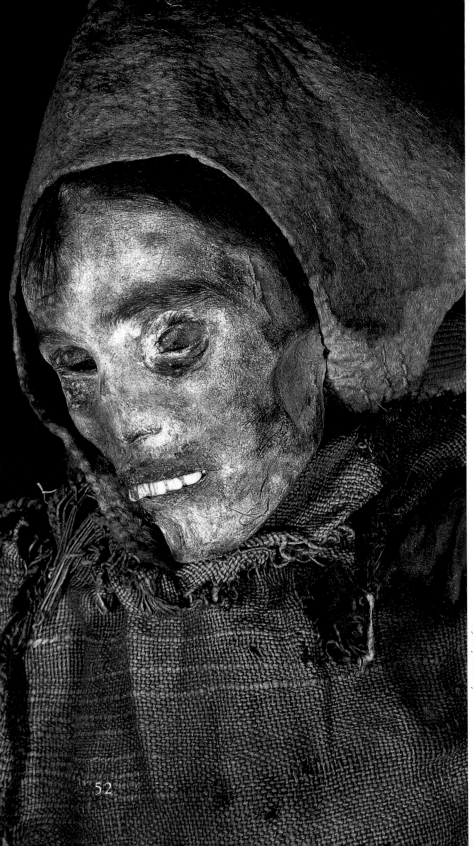

Chinese Mummy Mystery

Nestled north of a Chinese desert named Taklamakan (common interpretation: "You go in, but you don't come out") is the starkly remote town of Urumchi. Located in the Xinjiang region 1,600 miles east of Beijing, China's capital, Urumchi is not normally a stop for tourists—unless they're drawn to a really good mummy mystery.

What is the mystery in Urumchi? The mummies of Urumchi were found in China, so it was originally believed they were of Chinese descent. But the DNA evidence proved that, genetically, these mummified people were more closely matched to Europeans. Perhaps they were ancient settlers drawn to the famous Silk Road that ran from the Middle East to China.

Seven bodies are on display in the Urumchi Museum—a child and an adult in one room, and a child and four adults in another. Thousands of years ago, these seven people—who were naturally mummified by a combination of time, dry, hot winds, and salty soil—were laid to rest in three different places. Dressed in fine clothing of complicated weaves and crisp, dyed colors, the mummies—including the two children: Blue Bonnet Baby and the Qawrighul Child—offer many questions but few answers.

© Jeffery Newbury

Mystery surrounds mummies, like this female, who were discovered in the Chinese desert. DNA evidence proves that the mummies were more closely matched to people of European descent than of Chinese descent.

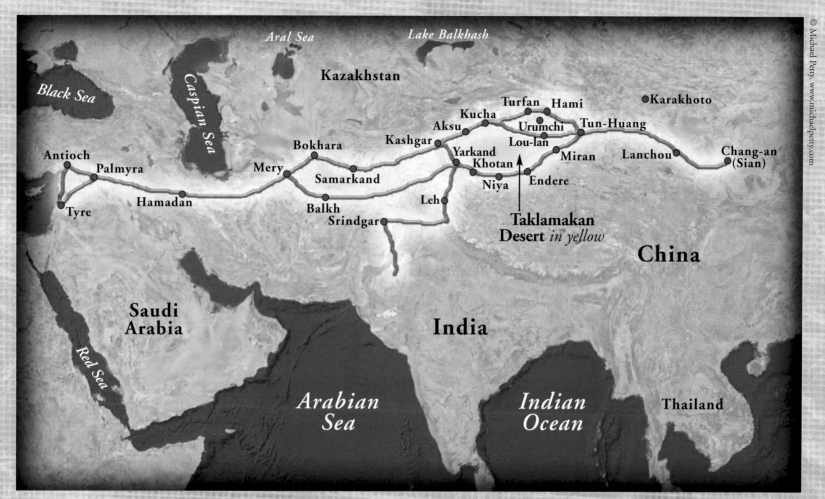

This representation of the Silk Road shows cities and routes throughout its history from the first century to about the fourteenth century.

What Was the Silk Road?

Imports and exports are a very common part of life in our modern, global community. We transport products made in one country to many other nations eager to buy them—and all in a matter of only days, or even hours. But it wasn't always so easy. Before the invention of cars, trains, or airplanes, traveling from one nation to another took a huge investment of time and money. On top of that, the way was difficult and dangerous.

Even so, brave individuals opened the trails for trade centuries ago. And the famous Silk Road was one of the first routes established for exchanging international goods between the Far East, the Middle East, and Asia. Travel along this five-thousand-mile-long road was done by caravans over land and by ocean vessels across the seas.

Longer than ever, the Silk Road is still in use today.

CHERCHEN MAN AND THE BLUE BONNET BABY

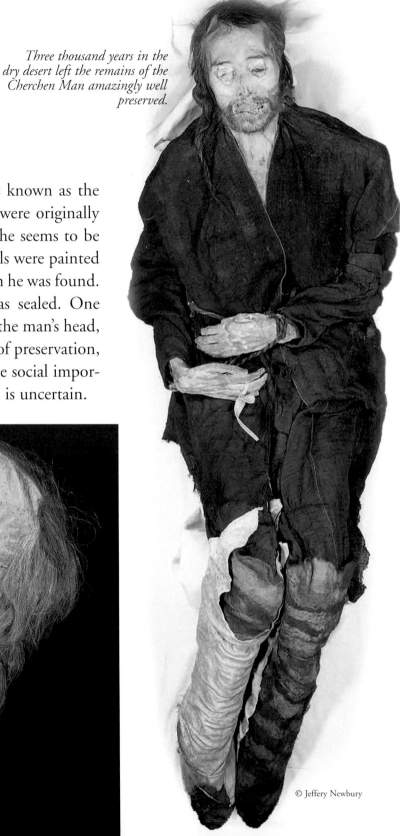

Three thousand years in the dry desert left the remains of the Cherchen Man amazingly well preserved.

One adult male who is housed at the Urumchi Museum is known as the Cherchen Man, after the village in which he and three others were originally found. Roughly fifty-five years old and six-feet, six-inches tall, he seems to be the head of household of this mummified grouping. Yellow swirls were painted on his face before he died and remained clear centuries later when he was found.

Three women were buried with him before the tomb was sealed. One woman, six-foot-tall in life, was buried lying horizontally above the man's head, like the top of a *T*. Based on her elaborate dress and her degree of preservation, experts believe she may have been the Cherchen Man's wife. The social importance of the other two women, lying just beyond the man's feet, is uncertain.

© Jeffery Newbury

Painted swirls from the time of his death are still visible on the Cherchen Man's face.

54

© Jeffery Newbury

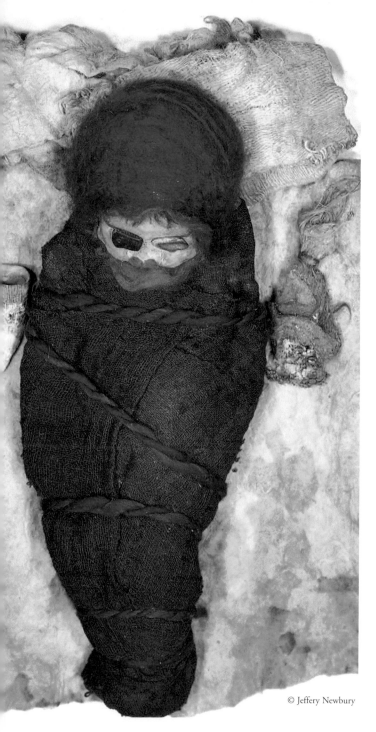

The four adults seem to have died as a result of the same common disaster or illness. Not long after this tomb was sealed, a three-month-old infant was buried in a small grave nearby. Now known as the Blue Bonnet Baby, this little one's gender is unknown.

Experts, including Dr. Elizabeth Wayland Barber, author of *The Mummies of Urumchi*, believe it was probably the child of the Cherchen Man and his wife. Why? Because the child was wrapped in a type of wool very much like that used to make the older man's wardrobe. And the same cord that held the Cherchen Man's hands in place also bound the Blue Bonnet Baby's brownish-red shroud. At the time of his or her burial, the child was gently placed on a clean, white felt blanket, and his or her head rested on another piece of white cloth stuffed with raw wool, forming a little pillow.

One clothing piece unique to the infant was a tiny cap—the inspiration for his or her nickname, "Blue Bonnet Baby." Still a vivid blue after three thousand years, the cap is trimmed in red, framing the little one's face. And peeking out of the cap are a few tiny shocks of light-brown hair. Two blue stones, nearly as brightly colored as the cap, cover the baby's eyes, and tufts of natural-colored wool dangle from his or her tiny nostrils. A burial shroud covers the baby's mouth. Next to the child were two personal belongings—a small animal-horn drinking cup and an ancient version of a baby bottle (made of a sheep udder).

Without CT scans or other detailed physical examinations, it's hard to know for sure, but Dr. Barber theorizes that the adults died first and that surviving friends or relatives tried to keep the infant alive, even without mother's milk to feed it, explaining the primitive bottle. When the baby passed away, the villagers reunited the family by burying the child next to its parents' main tomb.

© Jeffery Newbury

The Blue Bonnet Baby, although buried in a separate grave, is believed to be the Cherchen Man's child, because both were wrapped in the same kind of wool and bound by the same type of cord. Note the horn drinking cup on the left and remains of a sheep-udder "bottle" on the right.

THE QAWRIGHUL CHILD AND THE BEAUTY OF LOULAN

In about 2000 B.C., a thousand years before the Cherchen Man and his family died, two other bodies were laid to rest in two tombs further east in a village known as Loulan, located in the Qawrighul region. One of the mummies came to be known as the Beauty of Loulan because of her lovely facial features. The other, buried in a second tomb not far from her, was an eight-year-old who is simply called the Qawrighul Child.

This slight, even delicate, eight-year-old was wrapped head to toe in a finely woven shroud of light brown and darker brown that displayed his or her mother's skills as a weaver. Dr. Barber notes in her book that the weaving seems to have been crafted by a young woman just learning her craft. The cloth was held together with ten carved, wooden pins.

Also described in Dr. Barber's book was the careful way the Qawrighul Child was wrapped in the woven fabric. Strips of a darker textile framed the face, nestled by gentle folds, and the most complicated and beautiful fabric lovingly had been placed at the crown of the child's head.

Found nearby was the Beauty of Loulan, whose mummy enchanted China when she was discovered in the 1980s. A painting showing a possible reconstruction of her face hangs on the wall near her mummy in the Urumchi Museum. Dressed in leather moccasins and a leather skirt lined with animal fur, Beauty was prepared for the freezing Taklamakan Desert winters. Her outer wrap, held together with a wooden pin, was made of sheep's wool, suggesting she had access to domesticated animals. Her hand-stitched cap included a feather, but whether it was for decorative or other purposes is uncertain. Beside her head lay a woven bag lined with grains of wheat.

Another mummy found near this tomb had tools that were used to separate wheat grains from wheat chaff (the unwanted husk), which means that even four thousand years ago, these ancient people knew how to farm or trade for wheat, which they could use for nourishment.

© Jeffery Newbury

The clothing and accessories found buried with the Beauty of Loulan reveal that she was dressed for the cold winter in the desert and had access to agricultural items, such as livestock and grain.

56

The stunningly woven fabric in which the Qawrighul Child was carefully wrapped reflects that someone, probably the mother, lovingly prepared the child for burial upon his or her death.

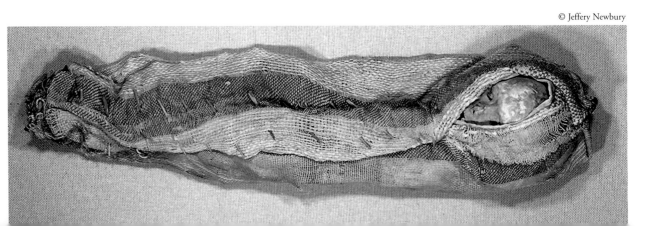

© Jeffery Newbury

KID MUMMIES FROM NORTH AMERICA

Unlike in South America, Egypt, Europe, and Asia, mummies are seldom discovered on the North American continent. When they do turn up, now and then, it is usually by accident. Hikers find them in rural caves. Construction crews turn them up while plowing through undeveloped ground. Suddenly the past comes face-to-face with the present.

When a mummy is discovered in the United States, an ethical conflict often arises, making it difficult for experts to study the mummy. Native American tribal leaders stand as strong advocates of the dead, determined to protect the people they consider their distant ancestors. These leaders want the dead left in peace after their spirits have left their earthly vessels, even if the human remains might have scientific value.

Even very ancient mummies that may not be genetically related to modern American Indian tribes are protected in the United States and are normally reburied after some basic scientific tests have been performed. But those few that have been available for study have shared amazing information about life in years gone by.

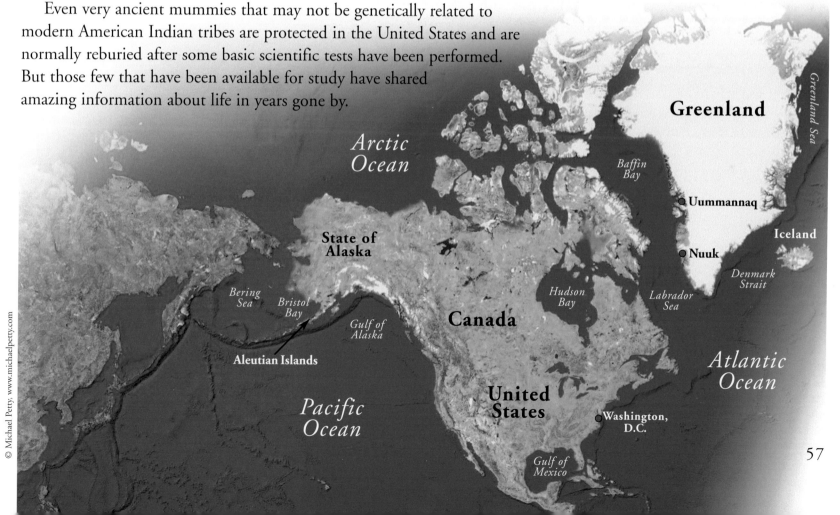

57

GREENLAND'S WOMEN AND CHILDREN

Something tragic happened about 550 years ago in the wilds of Greenland's Qilakitsoq settlement—an area that has long since been abandoned. Eight ancient Greenlanders, called Inuit, passed away and were laid to rest in two different burial caves. The frigid climate and freeze-drying winds preserved the bodies of six women and two children, until two brothers, Hans and Jokum Gronvold, stumbled on them in 1972 during a hunting expedition.

According to NOVA's documentary, *Ice Mummies*, the bodies had been buried one on top of the other with the youngest baby perched on top. The Gronvolds at first thought it was a doll—until they held it in their arms and saw it was an almost perfectly preserved ancient baby. The men gently replaced the tiny bundle and went to the police, who soon contacted Claus Andreasen, curator at the Greenland National Museum in Nuuk.

Andreasen was also moved when he saw the infant, whose tiny eyelashes were still intact. But it was one of the adult women who took his breath away. "One of the mummies that looked pregnant was lying with her hands on her stomach, in the way a pregnant woman would sit," he said. Of course, experts try to remain professional, but Andreasen and his team were only human. Overwhelmed by what they found, they had to take a break before they could finish preparing the mummies for transport.

When Danish forensic anthropologist Niels Lynnerup saw the mummified infant, he mirrored what the brothers must have felt. "The first time [you] are that close to the mummies, it really strikes you, the extraordinary degree of preservation of not just clothing but the tissue," he said in the documentary. "For instance, with the child mummy, it's as if he's looking at you with these wide-open eyes."

58

The near-perfectly preserved infant mummy found near the former Qilakitsoq settlement in Greenland appears doll-like, wrapped in fur.

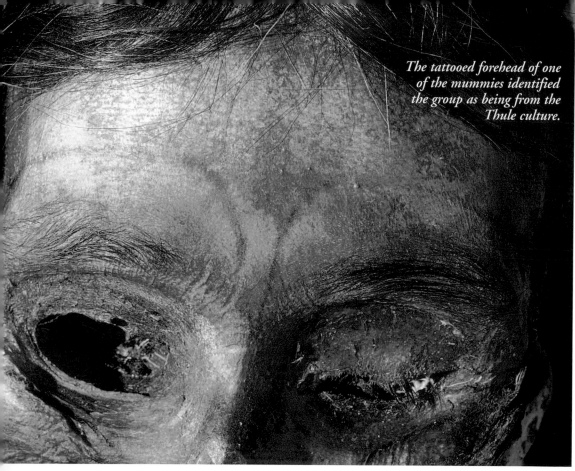

The tattooed forehead of one of the mummies identified the group as being from the Thule culture.

© Werner Forman Archive

A Safe Place to Rest

Why move these mummies at all? "Because the world is full of too many grave robbers," Andreasen said. They carefully moved the mummies from the caves to their new home at the Greenland National Museum.

Once the mummies had been secured at the museum, Andreasen and others began to investigate who these unlucky people may have been. Based on local history, their style of dress, and the burial location, these mummies most likely were members of the Thule culture, immigrants from Northern Canada who were once common to the area. The clothes also indicated these people probably didn't freeze to death. Dressed in hand-sewn, sealskin clothes with the fur facing inward, they were ready for the cold. So something else must have taken their lives.

Two of the women were older, their teeth ground down by years of processing sealskin into soft, flexible, waterproof cloth by chewing it. The other woman was young, in her late teens or early twenties. Perhaps she was the mother of the two child mummies: a four-year-old and another no more than six months old, both male.

Joined by Lynnerup, Andreasen and the Greenland National Museum team conducted scientific tests on the mummies to help solve the mysteries—including what had caused their deaths.

The tests revealed that these individuals were related to one another. Infrared cameras revealed something that might have been missed by the naked eye. The five older women had hand-stitched facial tattoos across their foreheads and on their chins, a Thule tribal tradition still practiced by some Greenlanders today. The stitched patterns were nearly identical, as was common among family members.

According to reports by author Jens Peder Hansen in his book, *The Greenland Mummies*, tests also proved one older woman had a malignant tumor at the base of her skull. A second older woman suffered with kidney stones. And the older child had a condition called Calve-Perthes disease, which caused him to limp and made him susceptible to other illnesses. Some of the mummies had signs of lung disease, the same kind of disease that today is caused by air pollution. Cooking and burning whale blubber lamps in a closed space probably caused the disease in these individuals.

One more question was left unanswered: Why were only women and children found here, but no adult men?

Inuit history tells us the Thule women spent days in their dome-shaped huts preparing animals skins, sewing, and caring for their children, while the men

© Mark J. Wilson

were hunting on the seas. Did the women and children starve to death waiting for food? The answer is no, according to Lynnerup. Evidence of food was found in the mummified stomachs, suggesting they had eaten before they died.

Another theory suggests they may have drowned at sea during a migration, but Andreasen and Lynnerup say it's doubtful. The clothing had no sign of tiny stones or sand embedded in the folds or fur, and the material showed no tears that would indicate a life-or-death struggle.

But even with DNA tests and CT scans, the causes of death weren't clear. Most likely a deadly illness or a collective case of food poisoning struck while the men were away. Most likely, they came home to discover their loved ones had died and then laid them to rest in the ancient caves.

Today the Inuit baby and two of the adult mummies are reverently displayed along with dozens of Inuit artifacts at the Greenland National Museum.

The rock graves at the site where the Greenland mummies and other skeletal remains were discovered remain mostly unchanged. Visitors respect the site as a burial ground, and the site is frozen most of the year, which makes it difficult to reach.

Mummies of Alaska's Aleutian Islands

From the mid-1800s to the mid-1900s, adventurers flocked to Alaska's Aleutian Islands to collect and document a new kind of mummy. Almost three hundred years ago, Aleutians (also known as Unangans) carefully prepared some of their dead, including individuals important to their group and some children.

The bodies of those chosen for mummification had their internal organs removed. The hollow space was then stuffed with dry grasses, and the body was carried to a freshwater stream. Currents of cool water dissolved and washed away all body fat.

Next the skin was softened with a fatty cream-like substance to make it flexible. Then the bodies were bound in a seated position with handmade cord, their knees draw up against their chests.

Dried in the sun, the bodies were next wrapped in layers of waterproof leather and other kinds of animal skins (including the feathered skins of birds) and hand-woven cloth. Once fully prepared, they were laid to rest in warm, volcanic caves for their trips to the afterlife.

It was in those caves that explorers hired by museums and private collectors found their new treasures. Dr. Harold McCracken was one of the explorers. He is mainly known for his work in excavating mummies and artifacts from the Aleutian Islands, including ancient toy polar bears carved from whale bone.

The Smithsonian's Museum of Natural History has thirty-six of the mummies in their collection, including mummified children.

(above) Dr. Harold McCracken examines one of the Aleutian mummies that he discovered.

(left) Once the Aleuts prepared their dead for mummification, they bound the bodies in seated positions, as these mummies were found in south-central Alaska.

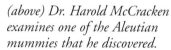

61

Civil-War-Era Teenager

Unearthing a cast-iron, Civil-War-era coffin with a mummy inside wasn't on the construction crew's schedule on Friday, April 1, 2005, in Washington, D.C. But that's exactly what happened. As they dug, the men heard the ring of metal against metal and discovered an astonishing relic from the past.

Shaped like an Egyptian sarcophagus and covered in layers of dirt and rust, DBT Development project manager Randy Boyd knew this casket was something old and rare. So, before the crew quit for the day, he had them place the heavy coffin into a seven-foot ditch inside security fencing and cover it with a blue tarp. They locked up the site and left, convinced the find would be safe.

On Monday, Boyd found that over the weekend teenage vandals had climbed the fence, thrown back the tarp, and pounded on the mysterious box, cracking the casket's faceplate and shattering the glass behind it. The damage was minor, but it allowed Boyd to see, not just a skeleton, but "a head with strands of blond hair, leathery skin, and a scarf wrapped around it," according to an April 7, 2005, report in the *Washington Post*.

Jane Freundel, a historian for Cultural Tourism D.C., said the once-upscale neighborhood had been near five Civil War hospitals in the 1860s. And the fact that this was an expensive Almond Fisk casket, patented in 1848, helped Freundel and other experts begin to piece together a possible profile of the person inside. Even so, much remained a mystery until the casket was opened—four months later.

In August 2005, a team from the Smithsonian Institute's National Museum of Natural History led by famed forensic anthropologist, Dr. Douglas Owsley and his associate Dr. Kari Bruwelheide, also of the Smithsonian, took on the challenge. Using electric drills, hammers, and chisels, the scientists pounded and prodded to break the ironclad seal that had made it possible to mummify the person in the first place. It may have seemed less than reverent, but, as Dr. Bruwelheide said in a National Public Radio (NPR) broadcast, "There's just no pretty way to do this."

This photograph of the construction of the U.S. Capitol building in Washington, D.C., was taken in the early 1860s, about the same time as the Civil-War-era teenager passed away and was buried in his Almond Fisk casket in a nearby neighborhood.

Once the lid was lifted, everyone remained silent as Dr. Owsley began to analyze what he saw. Because of the small size of the casket, he had expected the person inside to be a girl. But in very little time, he knew this was a mummified boy.

"He likely died around the age of thirteen," Owsley said on NPR, after assessing the size of the mummy and its clothing. "Nobody knows who this is," he continued. "This is our opportunity to help this person tell his story."

The Civil-War-era mummy of a young teenager was discovered by a construction crew. He was sealed in a cast-iron Almond Fisk casket, similar to the one shown here.

© Jason Meyers/ Museum of Funeral Customs

Many of the details gathered through an autopsy, CT scan, and DNA analysis will have to wait for the publication of an official scientific paper in 2007. Experts keep those facts hush-hush until they can make the findings official. In fact, no photos of the child mummy have been released, pending the publication of this report. But Dr. Owsley did share a few observations.

There was no obvious identification with the boy, but he seemed to be well loved and financially well to do. Of the fine burial clothing the teen wore, only the socks seemed to be factory made. The shirt, pants, vest (with a pocket), and even the undershorts were hand-stitched. A burial cloth was carefully draped and folded around the body. A scarf lay over his face.

There was some indication that the boy may have had pneumonia. The medical tests have since been conducted to confirm or discount this diagnosis, but again, mum's the word.

American University School of Communications *Alumni News* said Dan Sonnett was on hand to film the opening of the cast-iron time capsule, the autopsy, and the CT scan. His work has appeared on National Geographic and other documentary productions. So, in time, there may be a documentary about this find as well.

"When we go back in time, there is nothing you can think of in the archaeological record that can tell us more about a person—what his or her life was like—than examining the human remains," Dr. Owsley told NPR.

Until the official articles and film projects surface, this thirteen-year-old will remain something of a mystery. But what are a few more months when it comes to telling an American mummy's tale?

This image of a well-off teenage boy shows the type of finery the Civil War-era teenager might have worn.

MUMMIFICATION IS NOT ANCIENT HISTORY

Until now, our study of mummification has been a look back in time—an exploration of burial practices in the past. But does that mean there is no future for mummification? The answer is no, according to Utah businessman "Corky" Summum Bonum Amon Ra. Sometimes called the father of modern mummification (and formerly known as Claude Nowell), Ra has developed a process that he says captures and preserves the dearly departed—both humans and pets—in a way ancient Egyptians never imagined.

What is the process? The body is first placed in a sealed tank for several months in what Ra calls his "special preserving solution." When the body is removed, even a furry animal is so well preserved that its fur is still soft and natural, Ra says. The preserved person or creature's eyes reportedly look normal and healthy. Ra's process completely deactivates *rigor mortis,* or the stiffening of the body after death. "The bodies are preserved in the same condition they were in when they passed," Ra says. "And the process is permanent."

Next, the bodies are covered in a lanolin cream and wrapped in about thirty layers of gauze. A pine resin similar to that used by ancient Egyptians is used to coat the wrapped body, which is then covered in plaster and covered with gold leaf, gold that is beaten into very thin sheets. Finally, the mummy is placed in a Mummiform®, which is a sarcophagus made of quarter-inch-thick bronze, and the process is complete.

But perfect preservation comes at a high price. Pets like dogs and cats can be immortalized for $25,000 and up. Human beings invest between $67,000 and $350,000 for the licensed treatment. Hundreds of people have already made use of Ra's services, and even more have paid in advance to have their bodies preserved when they eventually pass away.

The reason for reviving a modernized version of the ancient ritual is not surprising. "Most clients who wish to be mummified dislike the idea of decomposing in the ground or being cremated," Ra says. "They prefer to be preserved eternally." They even have the option of taking some of their favorite possessions with them, tucked inside their wrappings.

For now, it's not all that common. But at Florida's Lynn University, students of mortuary science can take a certification class in Ra's specialized techniques. In time, mummification may become as common as headstones above ground.

A Mummiform® is the final resting place of Summum's mummies, including those of beloved pets.

CONCLUSION: WRAPPING THINGS UP

Centuries of human history have come and gone, and mummification has often been a choice of certain cultures all over the world. Hundreds of discoveries have given modern man an inside view of many different mummies—and a curiosity that gets stronger with each unearthing.

We ask ourselves two interesting questions:

1. Why have people tried to preserve their leaders and loved ones so often and in so many geographic places?

2. Why do we find it so fascinating to look at and study the mummies?

Experts and psychologists might give us a whole spectrum of answers based on studies and scientific facts. But I'm not an expert. So I'll share my opinions instead.

I think the answer to both questions is almost the same. We find ourselves nearly hypnotized by mummies because we all crave meaningful human connections. That yearning reaches beyond cultural differences. It is as common to all people as love or laughter or loss.

Whether living today or five thousand years ago, people search for love and purpose in their lives. We find these when we find a small group of special people—special to us, anyway. We try harder for a great coach. We admire a kind teacher. We fall in love. In other words, we connect.

Connection makes us happy. But losing connection makes us sad and afraid. So we try to build a bridge between life and loss, and mummification is a way humans have tried to maintain that connection.

The mummy of El Plomo boy serves as a powerful reminder of the connection between this life and the next that the Incas strongly believed in.

Mummified Incan children in Argentina and Peru gave up their lives to build a bridge between life and death for the people they loved. A boy king called Tut died at age seventeen, but lived on through his mummy and the valuable treasures stored in his afterlife tomb. Accidental mummies from Mexico, Greenland, and Italy draw hundreds of thousands of visitors every year.

It's okay to wonder and even shiver at the sight of these mysterious mummies. It's okay to put the book down after one page or to search for more books to help you find the answers to questions that weren't answered in this one. It's okay, because finding answers to your questions is all about connection, too. Taking a look at the world's mummies can help remind us that, past or present, every person has a story to tell.

MUMMY MISCELLANY

Dying to see a few mummies up close and personal? You don't have to travel to Peru or Egypt, China or Europe. If you check out this list of U.S.A. mummy resources, you just might find a mummy mystery in your own backyard.

ALABAMA

Anniston Museum of Natural History
800 Museum Drive
Anniston, AL 36207
(256) 237-6766
http://www.annistonmuseum.org/
• Two Egyptian mummies
• Plants and animals of Egypt
• X-rays of mummies

ARIZONA

Arizona State Museum
University of Arizona
1013 E. University Boulevard
Tucson, AZ 85721
(520) 621-6302
http://www.statemuseum.arizona.edu/
• Two mummified puppies
• Native American burial caves

CALIFORNIA

Museum of Man
1350 El Prado, Balboa Park
San Diego, CA 92101
(619) 239-2001
http://www.museumofman.org/
• Mummified falcon, Egyptian
• One Egyptian human mummy
• Famous Lemon Grove mummies
• Special Girl Scout Mummy Patch program

Rosicrucian Egyptian Museum & Planetarium
1342 Naglee Ave
San Jose, CA 95191
http://www.egyptianmuseum.org/
• One Egyptian mummy, female age 6

COLORADO

Denver Museum of Nature & Science
2001 Colorado Blvd.
Denver, CO 80205
(303) 322-7009
http://www.dmns.org/main/en/
• Two adult Egyptian mummies
• Animal mummies

GEORGIA

Michael C. Carlos Museum
Emory University
571 South Kilgo Circle
Atlanta, GA 30322
(404) 727-4282
http://www.carlos.emory.edu/
• Nine Egyptian mummies bought from Niagara Falls Museum in Canada

ILLINOIS

Field Museum of Natural History
1400 South Lake Shore Drive
Chicago, IL 60605
(312) 922.9410
http://www.fieldmuseum.org/
• "Inside Ancient Egypt" exhibit, twenty mummies
• Animal mummies

The Oriental Institute Museum
1155 East 58th Street
Chicago, IL 60637
(773) 702-9514
http://oi.uchicago.edu
• At least three Egyptian mummies
• Animal mummies

INDIANA

Joseph Moore Museum
Earlham College
801 National Road West
Richmond, IN 47374
(765) 983-1303
http://www.earlham.edu/biology/content/jmm/
• One Egyptian mummy, female

Wayne County Historical Museum
1150 North A Street
Richmond, IN 47374
(765) 962-5756
• One Egyptian priestess mummy

The Children's Museum of Indianapolis
3000 N. Meridian Street
Indianapolis, IN 46208
(317) 334-3322
http://www.childrensmuseum.org

KANSAS

Museum of World Treasures
835 E. First
Wichita, KS
(316) 263-1311
http://www.worldtreasures.org/
• Two Egyptian mummies

MASSACHUSSETTS

Museum of Fine Arts, Boston
Avenue of the Arts
465 Huntington Avenue
Boston, MA 02115
(617) 267-9300
http://www.mfa.org/
• Many Egyptian mummies, animals and human

Dinand Library's Archives & Special Collections
College of Holy Cross
1 College Street
Worcester, MA 01610
(508) 793-2011
http://www.holycross.edu/
• One Egyptian mummy, young girl named Tanetpahekau

MICHIGAN

Kalamazoo Valley Museum
230 N Rose Street
Kalamazoo, MI 49007
(269) 373-7990
(800) 772-3370
http://kvm.kvcc.edu/
• One Egyptian mummy, female adult
• One hundred artifacts and a facial reconstruction

MINNESOTA

Minneapolis Institute of Art
2400 Third Avenue South
Minneappolis, MN 55404
(888) MIA-ARTS
http://www.artsmia.org/
• One Egyptian mummy, Lady Teshat, a teenage girl

Science Museum of Minnesota
120 West Kellogg Boulevard
Saint Paul, MN 55102
(651) 221-9444
http://www.smm.org/
• One Egyptian mummy

MISSOURI

St. Louis Art Museum
One Fine Arts Drive, Forest Park
St. Louis, MO 63110
(314) 721-0072
http://www.stlouis.art.museum/
• One Egyptian mummy, Amen-Nestawy-Nakht, a priest of Amun

NORTH CAROLINA

North Carolina Museum of Art
2110 Blue Ridge Road
Raleigh, NC 27607
(919) 839-6262
http://ncartmuseum.org
• Two Egyptian mummy cases

OHIO

Boonshoft Museum of Discovery
3600 DeWeese Parkway
Dayton, OH 45414
(937) 275-7431
http://www.boonshoftmuseum.org/
• One Egyptian mummy

WASHINGTON

Burke Museum of Natural History & Culture
University of Washington
UW Campus at 17th Avenue NE & NE 45th Street
Seattle, WA 98195
(206) 543-5590
http://www.washington.edu/burkemuseum/
• One Egyptian mummy, female adult called Nellie (a CT scan revealed she had four feet)

BIBLIOGRAPHY

FOR FUTHER READING

For more information about all kinds of mummies, young and old, check out these books:

Barber, Elizabeth Wayland. *The Mummies of Urumchi.* New York: W. W. Norton, 1999.

Deem, James M. *Bodies from the Bog.* Boston: Houghton Mifflin, 1998.

Hansen, Jens Peder Hart. *Greenland Mummies.* Montreal, Quebec: McGill-Queens University Press, 1991.

Hawass, Zahi. *The Golden King: The World of Tutankhamun.* Washington, DC: National Geographic, 2004.

Hawass, Zahi. *Tutankhamun: The Mystery of the Boy King.* Washington, DC: National Geographic, 2005.

Pringle, Heather. *The Mummy Congress.* New York: Hyperion, 2001.

Reinhard, Johan. *Discovering the Inca Ice Maiden: My Adventures on Ampato.* Washington, DC: National Geographic, 1998.

Reinhard, Johan. *The Ice Maiden: Inca Mummies, Mountain Gods and Sacred Sites in the Andes.* Washington, DC: National Geographic, 2003.

BOOKS

Barber, Elizabeth Wayland. *The Mummies of Urumchi.* New York: W. W. Norton, 1999.

Brothwell, Don. *The Bogman and the Archaeology of People.* Cambridge, MA: Harvard University Press, 1986.

Buell, Janet. *Time Travelers: Greenland Mummies.* Brookfield, CT: Twenty-First Century Books, 1998.

Cockburn, Thomas Aidan. *Mummies, Disease, and Ancient Cultures.* Cambridge, MA: Cambridge University Press, 1998.

Deem, James M. *Bodies from the Bog.* Boston: Houghton Mifflin, 1998.

Hansen, Jens Peder Hart. *Greenland Mummies.* Montreal: McGill-Queens University Press, 1991.

Hawass, Zahi. *The Golden King: The World of Tutankhamun.* Washington, DC: National Geographic, 2004.

Hawass, Zahi. *Tutankhamun: The Mystery of the Boy King.* Washington, DC: National Geographic, 2005.

Pringle, Heather. *The Mummy Congress.* New York: Hyperion, 2001.

Vande Griek, Susan. *A Gift for Ampato.* Toronto: Groundwood, 1999.

Reinhard, Johan. *Discovering the Inca Ice Maiden: My Adventures on Ampato.* Washington, DC: National Geographic, 1998.

Reinhard, Johan. *The Ice Maiden: Inca Mummies, Mountain Gods and Sacred Sites in the Andes.* Washington, DC: National Geographic, 2003.

Shein, Max. *The Precolumbian Child.* Culver City, CA: Labyrinthos, 1992.

INTERVIEWS

Aftel, Mandy. Chemist. Interviewed June 26 and June 30, 2006.

Barber, Elizabeth Wayland, Ph.D. Professor of Linguistics and Archaeology and Author, Occidental College, Los Angeles, CA. Interviewed July 9, 2006.

Binneman, Johan, Ph.D. Curator of Archaeology, Albany Museum, South Africa. Interviewed July 7, 2006.

Cock, Guillermo, Ph.D. Catholic University, Lima, Peru; University of California, Los Angeles; Fowler Museum of Cultural History; Asociación Peruana de Etnohistoria. Interviewed June 2005.

Heflin, Tori D. Curator, Physical Anthropology, San Diego Museum of Man. Interviewed June 9, 2006.

Lynnerup, Niels, M.D., Ph.D. Laboratory of Biological Anthropology, Institute of Forensic Medicine, University of Copenhagen. Interviewed July 10, 2006.

Mair, Victor H., Ph.D. Professor of Chinese Language and Literature, Department of East Asian Languages and Civilizations, University of Pennsylvania. Interviewed July 7, 2006.

Mascali, Dario Piombino. Forensic Anthropologist, University of Pisa, Italy Interviewed July 3, 2006.

Owsley, Douglas W., Ph.D. Division Head for Physical Anthropology, Smithsonian Institution. Interviewed June 30, 2006.

Pieper, Peter, Ph.D. Forensics Expert, Dusseldorf, Germany. Interviewed July 14, 2006.

Reinhard, Johan, Ph.D. Explorer-in-Residence, National Geographic Society; Senior Research Fellow, The Mountain Institute; Author; Anthropologist. Interviewed May 30, June 5, and June 12, 2006.

Scott, Julie. Museum Director, Rosicrucian Egyptian Museum. Interviewed June 23 and 27, 2006.

BIBLIOGRAPHY

ARTICLES

Allingham, Winnie. "The Mystery of Inca Child Sacrifice." *Discovery Channel.com*, June 2, 2003.
http://www.exn.ca/Stories/1999/04/14/52.asp

Arriaza, Bernardo T. "Making the Dead Beautiful: Mummies as Art." *Archaeology*, December 16, 1998.
http://www.archaeology.org/online/features/chinchorro/

Braun, David. "Thousands of Inca Mummies Raised from Their Graves." *National Geographic News*, April 22, 2002.
http://news.nationalgeographic.com/news/2002/04/0410_020417_incamummies.html

Chamberlain, Ted. "King Tut Mummy Scanned, Could Solve Murder Mystery." *National Geographic News*, January 6, 2005.
http://news.nationalgeographic.com/news/2005/01/0106_050106_tut_scan.html

Cock, Guillermo A. "Inca Rescue." *National Geographic Magazine*, February 2005.

Gilman, Victoria. "Child Mummy Scanned at Stanford." *National Geographic News*, August 18, 2005.

Handwerk, Brian. "Accidental Mummies on Display in Mexico." *National Geographic News*, October 31, 2002.

Kovaleski, Serge F. (2005). Civil War-era casket vandalized in DC. *Washington Post*, 7 April.

Luongo, Michael. "500-Year-Old Frozen Bodies to be Displayed at Argentina Museum." *Bloomberg.com*, January 12, 2006
http://www.bloomberg.com/apps/news?pid=10000086&sid=azjRSlfmahQo&refer=latin_america

Martelle, Scott. (2006). Mysteries of the dead. *Los Angeles Times*, 30 April.

Ortiz, Fiona. "Chile's child mummy secrets unwrapped." *IOL*, November 27, 2005.
http://www.int.iol.co.za/index.php?set_id=1&click_id=

Philipkoski, Kristen. "Child Mummy Wows Egyptologists." *Wired News*, August 3, 2005.
http://www.wired.com/news/medtech/0,1286,68416,00.html?tw=wn_tophead_5

Roach, John. "Dozens of Inca Mummies Dicovered Buried in Peru." *National Geographic News*, March 11, 2004.

Sawyer, Kathy. (1999). Mummies of Inca children unearthed. *Washington Post*, 7 April.

Schuster, Angela M. H., "Andean Icewoman." *Archaeology*, January/February 1996.

---- "Inca Child Sacrifice." *Archaeology*. December 11, 1996.

Viegas, Jennifer, "Inca Tax Man Collected Child Sacrifices." *Discovery News*, May 30, 2005.

---- "Biblical-Era Child Mummy Resurrected." *Discovery News*, August 5, 2005.

Uncredited, "Seeking Clues to an Ancient Mystery." *University of Delaware Update*, April/May 2002.

Uncredited, "Interview with Guillermo Cock." *National Geographic News*, April 17, 2002.

Uncredited, "Mountain Mummy Is Baby." *BBC News*, April 16, 1999.

Uncredited, "Riddle of the Desert Mummies." *Discovery Channel*.

Uncredited, "Bodies of the Bogs." *Archaeology*, December 10, 1997.

Uncredited, "Tutankhamun Died of Gangrene, Say Experts." *IOL*, May 10, 2005.

Uncredited, "Construction Workers Unearth Civil War Coffin." *NABC4, District of Columbia, Maryland/Virginia*, April 6, 2005.

Uncredited, "Dan Sonnett . . . played a key role as videographer . . . on [Civil War] coffin study...." *American University Alumni News*, August 16, 2005.

VIDEOS

Greenland Mummies, Travel Channel - Transcript Courtesy of Clare Milward, Electric Sky Productions

Ice Mummies Box Set, NOVA

Ice Mummies, NOVA - Transcript
http://www.pbs.org/wgbh/nova/transcripts/2516frozen.html

Mysterious Mummies of China, NOVA

Mystery of the First Americans, NOVA - Transcript
http://www.pbs.org/wgbh/nova/transcripts/2705first.html

The Perfect Corpse, NOVA
http://www.pbs.org/wgbh/nova/bog/about.html

SGI Streaming Video, Sherit
http://www.sgi.com/streaming/sciences.html

Reconstructing Child Mummy, streaming video
http://www.fastfocus.tv/Media.aspx?id=230

AUDIO

The Bog Girl, BBC Women's Hour, April 27, 2005
http://www.bbc.co.uk/radio4/womanshour/2005_17_wed_04.shtml

Iron Coffin is Unexpected Time Capsule, NPR, August 7, 2004
http://www.npr.org/templates/story/story.php?storyId=4786001

BIBLIOGRAPHY

WEBSITES

Andes Expedition: Searching for Inca Secrets, National Geographic
http://www.nationalgeographic.com/features/97/andes/autopsy/intro.html

Assassination of King Tut, Discovery Channel
http://dsc.discovery.com/anthology/unsolvedhistory/kingtut/kingtut.html

Dr. Elizabeth Barber's Homepage
http://departments.oxy.edu/languages/barber.htm

Egyptians: BBC History
http://www.bbc.co.uk/history/ancient/egyptians/

Eternal Egypt (IBM)
http://www.eternalegypt.org/

Greenland Mummies/Our Heritage
http://www.ourheritage.net/Great_Adventures/Marine_Expedtions/Northwest_Passage/Uummannaq/Mummies.html

Ice Mummies, NOVA
http://www.pbs.org/wgbh/nova/icemummies/

Inuit Tattoo History
http://www.tattoo.dk/engelske/tattoo-history/inuit/e-inuit.htm

Tattoos of Early Hunter-Gatherers
http://www.vanishingtattoo.com/arctic_tattoos.htm

iScoliocis.com
http://www.iscoliosis.com/

Silk Road Foundation
http://www.silk-road.com/toc/index.html

Johan Reinhard's Journey
http://www.mountain.org/reinhard/

King's Capuchins Catacombs
http://members.tripod.com/~Motomom/index-3.html

Mountain Institute
http://www.mountain.org/

Mummies of China, NOVA
http://www.pbs.org/wgbh/nova/chinamum/

Mummy Tombs—James Deem
http://www.mummytombs.com/

Mystery of the First Americans, NOVA
http://www.pbs.org/wgbh/nova/first/claimjant.html

Mysterious Bog People
http://www.bogpeople.org/

Peatlands: History and Uses of Peat Moss
http://www.peatlandsni.gov.uk/history/fuel.htm

The Plateau: Official Website of Dr. Zahi Hawass
http://www.guardians.net/hawass/

RN PS Partnership—Yde reconstruction
http://www.rn-ds-partnership.com/home.html

Unwrap a Virtual Mummy: National Geographic Channel Inca Mummies
http://channel.nationalgeographic.com/channel/inca/

MUSEUM WEBSITES

Burke Museum of Natural History, Seattle, WA
http://www.washington.edu/burkemuseum

Kalamazoo Valley Museum, Kalamazoo, MI
http://kvm.kvcc.edu/

Metropolitan Museum of Art
http://www.metmuseum.org/special/SilverinAncientPeru/6.r.htm

Museo de Arqueologia, Antropologia e Historia del Peru
http://museonacional.perucultural.org.pe/ingles/elmuseo.htm

Museo Nacional de Historia Natural, Chile
http://www.mnhn.cl/

Museum of the Aleutians, Alaska
http://www.aleutians.org/

Museum of High Altitude Archaeology, Salta, Argentina
http://www.maam.org.ar/

NKA Exhibitions: The Qilakitsog Mummies, Greenland
http://www.natmus.gl/en/formidling/mumier/fmumier.html

Rosicrucian Egyptian Museum
http://www.egyptianmuseum.org/

San Diego Museum of Man, San Diego, CA
http://www.museumofman.org/

GLOSSARY

acllawasi — the residence or home for the girls chosen for special Incan duties

aclla — an individual girl selected to live in the acllawasi and fulfill special Incan duties; plural form *acllakun*

acsu — a long tunic worn by all Incan women and by Incan girls selected for sacrifice

advocate — to plead in favor of a person or group or a person who does this for a person or cause

alloy — a mixture of two or more melted metals or a metal with a nonmetal material

alpaca — a domesticated mammal of the camel family from Peru closely related to the llama

amulet — a charm or medallion, often worn on a necklace to protect the owner against evil, illness, or bad luck

anklet — an ornament worn around the ankle

annex — an additional structure or room meant to complement or add to another more central room

antechamber — a secondary room or chamber connected to the main chamber

anthropologist — a scientist who studies the history of ancient human beings

archaeologist — a scientist who studies ancient cultures by examining artifacts left behind

arsenic — an element poisonous to human beings and animals

artifact — an object created by a human being for a specific purpose

artisan — a person who is proficient or expert at a specific art form

base camp — a central camp from which explorers branch off to explore other nearby geographic landscapes

bespangled — brightly decorated with shining objects

bog — wet, soft, marshy ground, often with deep pockets of water

burial chamber — a room in which a person or people are entombed

burial cup — a drinking utensil left for deceased people to use in the afterlife

burial mask — a facial mask placed over the deceased to honor him or her

burial shroud — a cloth wrapped around a deceased human or animal

burro — a small donkey used as a pack animal

canopic jars — a container used to hold an Egyptian mummy's preserved organs

capacocha — an Incan ceremony in which children were sacrificed for the good of the empire

caravan — a company of travelers moving together toward a common destination

cartilage — an elastic tissue found at the nose, throat, ear, and other parts of the body

cartonnage — a death or burial mask

catalog (verb) — to carefully inventory, document, or keep track of items discovered or collected

Celts — an ancient European people who lived in central and western Europe during pre-Roman times

chaff — the dry skin coverings of grains and other seeds

chicha — an alcoholic drink made of corn

chonta — a palm tree with especially hard wood

chronicles — an account of events presented in chronological order

chuspa — a cloth bag used to hold coca leaves

conquistador — a Spanish conqueror or adventurer, especially one of those who conquered Mexico, Peru, and Central America in the 16th century

crook and flail — a crook is a tool, often used by shepherds, with a bend at the end; a flail is a whip

crypt — an underground burial room

CT scan — a diagnostic scan that produces a 3-D image on a computer screen

culmination — the highest, most important, or final point of an activity

decomposition — the chemical process by which organic material rots or breaks up

dysentery — a disease or infection in the lower intestines that causes severe diarrhea

Egyptologist — a scientist who studies the history, culture, language, and/or archaeology of ancient Egypt

embalming fluid — a liquid used to stop human tissue from decomposing

excavation — the act or process of digging up or removing earth from an archaeological site

facial reconstruction — the artful rebuilding of the structure of a face based on scientific facts

falsas cabezas — Spanish for "false head"

femur — the main bone in the human thigh

forensic anthropologist — an anthropologist who specializes in the study of things no longer living to determine the cause of death

GLOSSARY

forensic sculptor — an artist who prepares reconstructive 3-D models of persons or creatures no longer living

formalin — a solution used for preserving organic specimens

frostbite — damage to tissue caused by exposure to freezing conditions

funerary bundles — (See mummy bundles.)

hieroglyphics — a writing system that uses pictures or symbols to stand for words, especially used in ancient Egypt

huaca — a place in Peru considered holy or sacred

huaracas — a Peruvian sling used for hunting

hypoxia — a lack of oxygen in the body's tissue

indigenous — native to a specific geographic area

infant mortality rate — the rate at which babies who are less than one year of age die

ironclad seal — a completely airtight closure

intra-arterial — into the arteries of the vascular system

kayak — a traditional Inuit boat used for one or two people, often carved of wood and covered in animal skins

kero — an Incan wooden drinking cup

landmarks — familiar places unique to certain geographic locations

mace — a stick with an ornamental head that is used in ceremonies

maize — corn

malnutrition — a condition that results from not eating enough of healthy food

manganese — a brittle, grayish-white metallic chemical element

mantle — a loose, sleeveless cloak, such as a wrap or blanket

mummification — the preservation of human or animal's bodies, either by natural drying out or by a specific embalming process

mummy bundle — an Incan tradition of wrapping corpses and their personal objects in bundles in preparation for the afterlife

niche — a specialized compartment or small recessed space, often in ice or stone

paleopathology — the study of the nature, cause, and progress of disease

pathology — the study of diseases and the structural and functional changes produced by them

peat (sphagnum) moss — a moss that grows in wet places and whose partially decomposed remains form peat

pharoah — an Egyptian ruler

pilgrimage — a holy journey

pollen — tiny particles made by plants, also called microspores, carried by the wind that are necessary for fertilization

postmortem — after death.

quiver — a sleeve or holder for arrows

rainforest — a tropical wooded region with an annual rainfall of at least 100 inches

red ochre — red-colored iron ore often ground into a powder to make red paint

resin — naturally produced clear, yellow, or brown fluid that is not broken down by water and often dries into a hard, plastic-like substance

ritual — a ceremony or custom, often religious in nature

rudimental — basic, primitive, or simple; often imperfect

sarcophagus — a body-shaped burial case

scarab — a large beetle or the Egyptian trinket sculpted to resemble that beetle, which signifies resurrection

scoliosis — a condition that causes the spine to abnormally curve

sediments — layers of material deposited by wind or water

shantytown — a poverty-stricken, temporary community of shelters constructed from scrap materials

soldering — the act of using heat and molten metal to create a bond or union of metal objects

Southern Hemisphere — the half of the earth below the equator

Spondylus shell — the highly valued hard outer housing of a spiny oyster found in the Mediterranean Sea and off the coast of Ecuador

summit — a high-altitude location, often the highest attainable point

synthetic — artificially produced rather than found in nature

textiles — woven fabrics

treasury — a place where money or valuables are stored or kept

tuberculosis — an infectious disease that usually affects the lungs and is often fatal

tupu — an Incan pin used to hold pieces of clothing in place

ushutas — Incan sandals

vicuna — a pack animal closely related to the llama and alpaca

INDEX